THE BIBLE,

TEETOTALISM, AND DR. LEES.

A CONCISE

NARRATIVE, AND LECTURE:

WITH A

RECONSIDERATION OF THE ENQUIRY:

IS TEETOTALISM THE PLAIN TEACHING OF THE BIBLE?

BY

DAVID WILLIAMS,

OF GREAT HARWOOD.

1859.

PREFACE.

The Author of the following pages regrets that there should have been any necessity for publishing them. He is aware that a higher order of literature is needed to advance the intelligence and morality of the present age: and he would not have troubled the public with such observations as are here thrown together, except for the purpose of repelling an influence, which might threaten to interfere with the spread of religious principle, in a particular locality. Doubtless, it is very pleasant with some natures to cherish a feeling of vindictiveness, when any trivial opposition is apparent, or even suspected: but to the faithful expounder of God's Word, there remains no alternative, but honestly to declare what he believes to be the plain teaching of that *Word*. The flame of resentment may burn lurid, as it glowed when freedom of thought and private judgment were trampled out amid the fires of the sixteenth century; but whether we or our opponents speak the truth, it is a consolation to know that that truth shall be finally victorious. The writer pleads no exemption from the infirmities which are too common with mankind, nor does he boast of any authority in virtue of office. If any should suspect a want of charitable feeling, or a deficiency of argument in what is here given to the world, he must at least crave the indulgence of those who may reflect upon the arguments and epithets to which a reply is ventured.

The lecture which is embodied, pp. 20—39, was not intended at the time of its delivery for the eyes of the public. But when the lecturer found that it was to be publicly opposed, he deemed it advisable to publish, as nearly as possible, according to the form in which it had been spoken; and he has felt it needful now to adhere to an exact copy of the first impression. A judgment may thus be more accurately formed as to the value of certain criticisms which have been bestowed upon it. Although the writer could have wished to rewrite some parts, where there are manifest imperfections in arrangement and style, there is nothing in the lecture, so far as he is aware, which is untrue in fact, or wrong in argument.

May genuine Religion, including the principles of true Temperance, soon gladden our world with the utterance of all that is charitable, holy, and true! "Let us not therefore judge one another any more: but judge this rather, that no man but a stumbling block or an occasion to fall in his brother's way. ....Let not then your good be evil spoken of: for the kingdom of God is not meat and drink; but righteousness, and peace, and joy in the Holy Ghost."

CONTENTS.

PART I.

INTRODUCTORY.—Value of temperance—Need of consistent advocacy—Teetotalism—Charity—Who shall rebuke?—Benefit of abstinence—Individual experience—Alcohol as a medicine—Medicines sometimes injurious—Testimony of Religion and Science—Advice to the young—Cultivation of an enlightened and sanctified judgment—Principles of the Divine Word.

(pp. 9—14.)

PART II.

TEETOTAL TACTICS.—Dr. Lees' visit to Harwood—Subject of lecture—Design—What kind of Teetotalism is taught in the Bible?—Progress of the enquiry—Agitation—Who is the author of the Reply?—Unsound argument not needed for the defence of Teetotalism.

(pp. 15—19.)

PART III.

LECTURE.—*Is Teetotalism the plain teaching of the Old Testament?*—The enquiry important—What was forbidden to the Jews?—Christian liberty—Law for Priests and Nazarites—Definition of the Hebrew *yayin*—How used in the Old Testament—'Wine is a mocker'—*Yayin* intoxicating—Forbidden at specified times—Permission to use wine and strong drink—Definition of the Hebrew *shechar*—Testimony of Eadie's Bible Cyclopædia—The Bible does not enjoin Teetotalism upon all—It condemns drunkenness—The Israelites drank no wine in the wilderness—Melchizedek—Abraham—Noah—The Rechabites—Moral instructions enforced by their example—Daniel—Teetotalism in harmony with the Bible—Symbolism of Ps. lxxv. 8—Symbols variously interpreted—Dregs of the cup of wrath—Red wine—Drink offerings in the Temple—Wine the symbol of gospel blessings—Prov. xxiii. 31—Meaning of the expression, 'Look not upon the wine'—Danger connected with some kinds of food—Duty of Christians to be frugal and temperate.

(pp. 20—39.)

Part IV.

REMARKS ON THE REPLY.—The beginner of the controversy—Distinction between Bible teaching and harmony—Definition of Teetotalism—' Alcohol a bad article'—Wisdom of abstinence—' Alleged discrepancy'—' Galilei's rebuke'—' Substitution and perversion of terms'—' Proposition to be debated'—' Intoxicating drink a bad thing'—' Teetotalism, the observance of the law of food'—' Practised by individuals and societies under Divine sanction'—'A physiological law'—A Divine remedy'—' Preparation for spiritual life'—' Originally inspired'—' The manufactured proposition'—' Ruse of the cuttle-fish'—' Stern rebuke'—' Perversion of placarded title'—' Authorised version of the Bible'—Heathen authorities—' Perverse ingenuity'—Dr. Lees as an advocate for temperance—' Theological blundering'—' Jewism not Gentilism'—Teetotalism founded on reason—'Nothing unclean of itself'—' Wine wherein is excess'—Applications of the term *yayin*—' Philological knot'—Deductions of science—' Bibbler's philology'—' Physiology of Teetotalism'—Wines alcoholic—As described by classical writers—How to preserve grape-juice unfermented—Quotations from Pliny—Varieties of ancient wines—Plutarch—*Sapa* and *defrutum* of the Romans—' Appeal from ignorance to ignorance'—' Cranial opacities'—' Is grape-juice wine or not ?'—' *Tirosh* not *yayin*'—What is wine ?—Quotations from authorities—Syrup not wine—' Content with ignorance'—Dr Lees on the contents of Walton's Polyglot—' Verbalism more pitiable than quibbling'—' Blasphemy'—Wine mixed—Wealth a mocker—' Limitation of propriety'—' A little learning a dangerous thing'—The Hebrew *hhemer*, Isa. xxvii. 2—Wine the symbol of wrath and blessing—Scott, the Commentator, as an advocate of Teetotalism—' Pillar of absurd consistency'—' Defence of the opium traffic'—Various significations of symbols—' Evil consequence' of excess—Water an emblem of destruction and purification—Fire, a symbol of Divine Love and Wrath—' Just so with wine'—Could the ancient Jews detect Alcohol ?—'Symbol-ology'—Boiling the wine—Miller on the use and value of Alcohol—True source of the evil—Is vegetarianism plainly taught in the Bible ?—Blessing and bane—' Who hath woe ?'—' Drugged *mesech*'—Special rules for special circumstances—A dilemma—' Eye in the cup'—' Imbecility'—Distinctness of inspired utterances—Turkish morality and logic—Implication and plain teaching—' Self-denial'—The Hebrew *raah*, and Greek *scopeo*—' Most righteous Nemesis'—' Look not upon the wine *with desire*'—An emphatic denial, and a sturdy affirmation—New Testament teaching concerning Teetotalism—' Critical theory'—Greek words, *egkrateia*, *nephalios*, *nepho*, *me paroinos*—Dr. Lees' admission—Bible condemns gluttony, drunkenness, and all intemperance.

(pp. 40—131.)

"Who seeth not now the miserable estate, whereinto men are brought by these foul, filthy monsters, gluttony and drunkenness? The body is so much disquieted by them, that, as Jesus, the Son of Sirach affirmeth, *the insatiable feeder never sleepeth quietly, such an unmeasureable heat is kindled, whereof ensueth continual ache and pain to the whole body.* And no less truly is the mind also annoyed by surfeiting banquets: for sometimes men are stricken with frenzy of mind, and are brought in manner to near madness; some wax so brutish and blockish, that they become altogether void of understanding. It is a horrible thing that any man should maim himself in any member: but for a man of his own accord to bereave himself of his wits, is a mischief intolerable."—HOMILY AGAINST GLUTTONY AND DRUNKENNESS.

"*The proper* PLACE *of alcohol for man's use is as a medicine.* Let men put and keep it there. Its power then is both great and good.

"Let them regard it no longer as an article of ordinary diet; for wholesome, real food it is not, and power as such it has none.

"Let them beware of it as a luxury; for though its power as such be great, it is often grievous. And, looking to the exigencies of the present time, let them resolve, in God's strength and in God's name, to deny themselves what to the man in health is *but* a doubtful luxury at the best, and is shown by sad experience rather to become 'a mockery, a delusion, and a snare.' 'Wine is a mocker, strong drink is raging; and whosoever is deceived thereby is not wise.'"

ALCOHOL: *its place and power, by* J. MILLER, F.R.S.E.

PART I.

INTRODUCTORY.

TEETOTALISM has become a power in the world. It is a fact which none can dispute, that its advocates have unfurled a banner, around which thousands have rallied to assert their freedom from the debasing usages, and the abominable crimes of Intemperance. Honour to the men who, with honest hearts, and unswerving purpose, have gone forth to do battle in the cause of humanity—who have gone into the fetid atmosphere of moral evil where debauchery and lust have been uncontrolled by any sense of virtue, and snatched from the contagion immortal souls, who are destined to live for ever in the light of God. May the time soon come when men shall every where do honour to the consistent advocates of Truth and Temperance.

It were vain to think, however, that every man deserves to be crowned, who with impassioned energy pleads the cause of either Temperance or Religion. There are, doubtless, many advocates of the one and of the other, whose claims to the gratitude and respect of mankind may be considered as very superficial. The greed of gain, and the little pride of speech, which are satisfied by the display of some rhetorical power, furnish an ample reward for all the effort which they are at in catering for the popular taste.

The writer of this pamphlet has been particularly impressed with the necessity of extreme vigilance in the Church of Christ respecting the mode in which Temperance ought to be advocated. Teetotalism, he would repeat, has become a fact and a power in the world.

Ministers of the Gospel, Sabbath-school Teachers, Tract Distributors, Visitors of the Sick, and all who have to do with the dissemination of Scripture truth, must see in this fact, and in this power, something which claims their thoughtful attention. But is there not danger in some cases of attaching undue importance to this principle? Is it not to be lamented that some, who once confessed that "the Gospel is the power of God unto Salvation," and who still adhere to this form of words, have found their zeal diminished, and their usefulness impaired in the service of Christ, through an all-absorbing interest in the spread of Teetotal principles? If I may express my convictions honestly with regard to Teetotalism, I believe that it is something like a good quiet horse, that will do its work very well, if it is not over driven to its death. To Teetotal advocates I think it may be very properly said: Have patience! Give it time! Do not make a god of it; nor put it altogether in the place of religion. If Clericus cannot see things exactly in the same light as Doctor Philosophicus, that is no reason why Doctor Philosophicus should call Clericus an impudent blunderer; for such a method of argument may only show to the world that a diploma, like alcohol, may sometimes make a man forgetful of his proper self. Nothing will more entirely disgust the more thoughtful of the community than the arrogance which will tolerate no opposition, except with torrents of invective and abuse. We may be sure that neither friends nor enemies to the cause of Teetotalism will be made any the better by the lofty interdicts of some, who appear to think that all the harmonies in the universe must revolve around their one idea. I believe that large numbers have been already alienated from the advocacy of Teetotálism by the pretentious reviling of some of its professed supporters.

Doubtless some of our very violent friends will observe that, if Ministers, and other professing Christians choose to oppose Teetotalism, they ought to be reviled. In some instances, perhaps, their conduct may be injudicious: but who is to revile them? There are now, as there have been in times past, many godly men, though they have not professed the principles of Teetotalism; and their usefulness has been of a higher order, than many can comprehend. Such may say: "Let the righteous smite me; it shall be a kindness: and let him reprove me; it shall be an excellent oil, which shall not break my head." But if Shimei curse, "so let him." The revilings of the Reviler will never break the head of a man who is conscious that he has God and truth on his side; but they will rebound with terrible force and precision on the Reviler himself, and may be altogether unprofitable to his associates.

If Teetotalism be founded on fact, it shall prevail in spite of the opposing influence of its most injudicious professors, or its most sturdy opponents. There can be very little doubt, I think, that the principle of abstinence from intoxicating drink is, in multitudes of cases, most beneficial. With very many it is even necessary to the preservation of health and morals. And I am strongly of opinion that all, who have at heart the welfare of their fellow men, will do well to display their philanthropy by refraining from all kinds of strong drink, except for medicinal uses. But it may be expected that the writer should candidly tell the world whether he himself is a Teetotaller or not. It may displease many to know that at the present he does not profess to be a total abstainer. He has been a Teetotaller for years, even to the extent of entire abstinence: he has travelled many a weary mile over rough roads, and in dark nights, for the sake of giving Teetotal lectures, and addresses: he has gladly entertained, and that frequently, honoured friends and advocates of the cause of Temperance, and has felt his heart drawn towards them as brethren well-beloved: he has signed in favour of the Maine liquor law, and advocated what is well known to some as a Permissive bill: and, were it not that he feels bound by a certain peculiarity of constitution to use medicinally that which he could not recommend as an ordinary beverage, he would prefer on every account to be a total Abstainer still.

I know very well that it is customary to condemn this free and open kind of confession: and I may be asked: what good end can be answered by telling every one what is my practice, if it be not that of a perfect Teetotaller? To this I reply, truth is always more valuable than falsehood or hypocrisy. It is assumed by some that the doctrines of Teetotalism repose on the broad basis of physiological facts. That there are legitimate principles, as expounded by the Advocates of Teetotalism, which are so founded on fact, I am well assured. But, that we may either know the facts, or build up doctrines, which shall be permanent, and powerful, because they are true, we must be attentive to the testimony of individual experience. I have seen the printed declaration of Abstainers, who have shown that they are better without the use of Alcoholic drinks. I accept their testimony as most valuable in favour of total abstinence; and am led to think that in the great majority of instances, total abstinence is attended with the best results. At the same time, I believe that there are cases in which it would be injurious to health, and morally wrong, not to take what most physicians would prescribe in such cases, viz., an Alcoholic medicine.

But why plead for this as a medicine? Is it true that any deny it as such? It is well known that some will not allow the right to touch, or taste it, in any circumstances. In itself, they say, it is bad; and in no instance can it be of the slightest benefit. Whether the amount of importance attaching to their declaration be regarded as great or small, I think it right that they who think differently should speak their thoughts honestly. For the sake of Teetotalism itself, as well as for the interests of True Religion, it may be exceedingly desirable to establish this much, at least; that our Ministers, and Sabbath School Teachers, and others, who think that they have a right to judge for themselves, may assert their liberty of conscience; not by becoming little-drop drinkers, nor bibblers, nor boozers, according to the objectionable sense in which these words are usually understood; but by using *rationally* and *wisely*, as a medicine, that which, by multitudes of the most intelligent, is really considered a blessing. Some will object that Alcoholic medicines are frequently administered where they are not beneficial, but really injurious; and that in some instances where they were given to prolong life, they have in reality been the means of shortening it. That may be admitted. And the same may be said of other medicines. Yet those medicines continue to be administered, and very properly so, in some cases.

But is not the use of any Alcoholic drink, even as a medicine, dangerous, inasmuch as the medicinal use may lead to the ordinary dietetic use, and this again to a thorough abuse by indulgence in excessive potations? Perhaps so. But there is absolute safety nowhere but in the principles of true Religion, and the preserving grace of God. Teetotalism is only a safe guard against the sin of Drunkenness *so long as a man is* a Teetotaller. If, however, there be a proper medicinal use, it may, in some cases, be wise to adopt it: and *while one confines himself* to the proper medicinal use, he is as safe as the more rigid Teetotaller, who will not taste intoxicating drink under any circumstances. In fact, the path of right is always the safest, both physically and morally: and, if we know what this is, it will be the truest heroism and philanthropy to walk straight forward in this one path which Science and Religion unite to distinguish as the path of right. But, surely, as I would know what this is, I am not at liberty to please a few by discarding the testimony of the great bulk of scientific men and Theologians, and the use of my own reason and observation.

But here I feel it my duty to recommend as strongly as I can, the practice of general abstinence. I firmly believe that the cases are not of very frequent occurrence in which Alcoholic stimulants are either necessary or desirable. Let the young, especially, be careful to keep as far as possible out of harm's way. To all, the injunction should be addressed with the utmost earnestness: "Watch, and pray, that ye enter not into temptation." I believe that there are many instances in which persons are deceived by a conviction that they require what they would be really better without. The evidence should be very unmistakeable with me as to the desirableness of taking that, the abuse of which has led to the ruin of thousands, blasting their hopes for time and for eternity. But I cannot conceal from myself, that almost every gift of God's bounty has been abused by the corrupt devices and desires of men. Even the ministration of the gospel, while it is represented as "the savour of life unto life" in them that are saved, is declared to be "the savour of death unto death" in them that perish. But above the cries of the wandering and the lost, and amidst much strife and contention as to the way in which these are to be reclaimed, I hear the small voice of conscience, telling me that my defence is of God; and that health of body, and efficiency of action, imperatively demand that, in subservience to the law of God, I should obey the dictates of my own judgment, though confronted by the frowns or the menaces of all the societies in the world. Let Christians of every name be earnest in securing an enlightened and sanctified judgment: let that judgment be guided by Truth and Religion: above all, let it be regulated by the principles of God's word: let its decisions be formed in a spirit of humble prayer, and with a view to the highest interests of mankind in general. Then, as habits of enlarged thought, and enlarged Christian principle are induced, shall Christians feel that, in the fullest sense, their defence and security is of God. " *Add to your faith virtue; and to virtue knowledge; and to knowledge temperance; and to temperance patience; and to patience godliness; and to godliness brotherly kindness; and to brotherly kindness charity. For if these things be in you, and abound, they make you that ye shall neither be barren nor unfruitful in the knowledge of our Lord Jesus Christ; but he that lacketh these things is blind, and cannot see afar off, and hath forgotten that he was purged from his old sins. Wherefore the rather, brethren, give diligence to make your calling and election sure: for if ye do these things, ye shall never fall; for so an entrance shall be ministered unto you abundantly into the everlasting kingdom of our Lord and Saviour Jesus Christ.*"

PART II.

TEETOTAL TACTICS.

In a Lancashire village, pleasantly situated on the northern edge of the Cotton manufacturing district, there are living at the present time a number of individuals who are staunch professors of Teetotalism. For the most part, they are prospering in their way, and some of them have cause to be thankful for the combined influences of Christianity and Teetotalism. There seems, however, on the part of a few, a strong determination to inveigh most vehemently against the use of strong drink, whether as a beverage or a medicine. Several of the best lecturers on their favourite topic have been employed to enlighten the people of Harwood; and to some of these the writer has listened with pleasure, though, at times, with feelings of great sorrow when christian men and christian ministers have been grossly caricatured. But I have felt it my duty, so far as possible, to aid what for some time appeared to me a legitimate method for the suppression of Intemperance. Lately, however, the avowal of the Curate, and the Minister, that they are not Teetotallers has given grave offence. It was in vain for the latter to plead that he could not conscientiously profess to be an Abstainer while under an evident necessity to use, though at considerable intervals, and in very minute quantities, what some object to as in itself a bad thing. He has been wrathfully informed by a youthful aspirant that he is inconsistent; and very shortly after, the township was told by printed notices that Dr. Lees was engaged to lecture in the Independent School Room on two successive evenings, with the following as the subject of his second lecture: "*Teetotalism the plain teaching of the Bible.*" But the Independent School Room had not been let for such a purpose. Indeed, no word was given either to the Minister, or Deacons, or Trustees, who should have been consulted about the letting of the room, that it was wanted on those evenings. Moreover, it was well known that while the Minister had sought, in every legitimate method, to advocate the practice of abstinence, he decidedly opposed the notion of Teetotalism being taught in the Bible. While, therefore, Dr. Lees was permitted to have the room on the former of the evenings specified, it was not allowed that he should appear to give battle to the Minister on the ground occupied by his own place of worship. The Teetotallers were therefore requested to seek for the delivery of the second lecture a more appropriate spot. The Wesleyan Chapel was obtained instead: and there the Doctor delivered his second lecture; "*Teetotalism the plain teaching of Scripture.*"

It may be needless to ask; what was the probable design of that lecture, or, as it has been happily expressed, the "perversion of its placarded title." Of course, the inference would be obvious, that if Teetotalism be the plain teaching of the Bible, then every Christian man, woman, and child, in the country, is bound by the law of God to be a Teetotaller. Teetotalism is thenceforth put on a level with Christianity itself. And, I suppose, such an astute process of reasoning might be adopted in some parts as the following. Teetotalism is the plain teaching of the Bible; Christianity is the plain teaching of the Bible; wherefore, according to the logic of Dr. Lees, who assumes that things which harmonize are identically the same, Teetotalism and Christianity are one and the same thing. And here are the corollaries which some might be disposed to draw from this: Teetotalism and Christianity being one and the same thing, he who is a Teetotaller is a good Christian, and no man is a Christian who is not a Teetotaller. Certainly, if Teetotalism be the plain teaching of the Bible, no Christian Minister should continue to hold his office as a Minister, who does not practise Teetotalism.

But seriously, if Teetotalism be the plain teaching of the Bible, the discoverer of this fact should enlighten us as to the kind of

Teetotalism which is there taught. Let us have the thing clearly defined. Does the Bible allow the medicinal use, or does it not? Does it require the signing of a pledge in favour of abstinence, or not? If it does, then which is the orthodox pledge? Does it, or does it not allow the use of those weak wines which many Teetotallers feel themselves at liberty to take? Albeit we are not sure that some Alcohol does not lurk therein. According to the scriptural teaching, may fermented yeast or leaven be used in bread, and brandy be smuggled first into the kitchen, and then into the sauce, or not? Now, in the vicinity of a certain order of minds, all this is really important to be known: for some of our old fashioned christians are not always ready to rejoice in the reproaches of those who insist that we must take the Teetotalism of the Bible, without telling us what it is. At least, if we are to receive this Scriptural Teetotalism, let us see what it means. If we are to be Nazarites, we must not eat grapes: if we are to be like the sons of Jonadab, we should dwell in tents: if we are to be in all respects like Daniel we must be content with a vegetable diet, and be limited in our drinking habits to pure water. Are we to abstain after their fashion? I affirm with all sincerity, that I do not wish to cavil, nor to find fault with any of my Teetotal brethren. But I formerly thought that Teetotallers allowed the use even of Alcohol, especially if very much diluted, where bodily infirmity seemed to require it. I am not anxious, it is true, to play the part of him who, in trying to please every body, pleased nobody, and lost his ass to the bargain. But as at the *pons asinorum* many dull scholars stick, so am I fast here. What sort of a bridge is this Bible Teetotalism?

For various reasons, which it is needless to assign, I have been particularly desirous not to enter into controversy with Dr. Lees on any subject. I was precluded by other engagements from hearing his lecture on the plain teaching of Scripture. But I felt it my duty to examine the matter very carefully for myself, and to lay the result of my enquiries before the people. The feeling of mutual respect, and brotherly love, which should always subsist between ministers of different evangelical communions, were of great assistance here; for the Rev. R. H. Wilkinson, Curate of

Harwood, feeling very much as I felt myself respecting the question at issue, promised that, if I would take the teachings of the Old Testament, he would take the teachings of the New. We, therefore, agreed to give a course of two or three lectures between us on the one enquiry: "Is Teetotalism the plain teaching of Scripture?" The Teetotallers resolved to make the most of my second lecture. A reporter was engaged to write it as it was delivered: and an agent of the United Kingdom Alliance was advertised immediately to deliver a lecture at the Wesleyan Chapel in reply. About the same time, I heard that Dr. Lees was to visit Harwood a second time, in order to make good his own statements, and to upset mine. Under these circumstances I thought it the safer course to publish my lecture in full, that it might be known what I had really said to provoke so much opposition. My friend, Mr. Wilkinson, decided on publishing at the same time a statement of his views, which were published in "a letter to the Teetotal Society of Great Harwood." No sooner were our pamphlets in print than the following advertisement appeared in a local Newspaper :—" Will be ready in a few days, an Exposure of the Rev. D. Williams' lecture, entitled 'Is Teetotalism the plain teaching of the Bible?' evincing its falseness—its perversions—its false criticisms, and its blunders. Published for the Great Harwood Temperance Society. This will be followed almost immediately by a similar exposure of the Rev. Mr. Wilkinson's impertinent letter addressed to the Society. To be had from all Booksellers, &c." This of itself is a singular specimen of Teetotal Temperance, and a mode of discussion which, for the honour of True Temperance, I hope is not very frequently adopted even among the most ultra of Teetotallers. Week after week, first in the columns of one paper, then of another, was this precious advertisement fulminated for more than a month; and even after the "Exposure" was out, the advertisement was too good to be lost sight of, so for at least two weeks after, came the same reprint; "Will be ready in a few days, an Exposure, &c."

By whom the "Exposure" is written I will not say, as the Author does not declare his name: but it is very generally understood that Dr. Lees has found it convenient to publish anonymously. The internal evidence which is furnished in the pamphlet leaves but little doubt upon my own mind as to its real Author. But if that be Dr. Lees, it is astonishing how any man could write thus of himself and his own writings. The pamphlet is entitled, "Teetotalism plainly taught in the Bible," and is said to be "a Reply to the Lecture and Letter of the Rev. D. Williams and Rev. R. H. Wilkinson, of Great Harwood." I shall not wait here to characterize it. Those who can receive it as a very sensible and judicious reply in favour of a newly discovered fact, let them receive it. It may be a wonder to many, however, that such men as Owen, and Howe, and Doddridge, and Scott, and all our eminent commentators, have always been in the dark about this, if it be true, that Teetotalism is plainly taught in the Bible.

It will be of no service to strive for the advancement of Teetotal principles, nor of any other principles, by a fraudulent sophism, which shall be backed by wholesale misrepresentation and abuse. For the credit and success of all that is good, the sooner a fallacious argument is exposed the better. Teetotalism, as practised and advocated by some of the best men of the age, requires no sham supports; and he who seeks to prop it up with statements which are untrue, inflicts upon the cause of genuine Temperance a serious injury. If Teetotalism be, as some of its advocates say it is, the plain teaching of the Bible, the sooner it is known the better: but, if it be not, I protest against the practise of flinging gibes and insults against Ministers of the Gospel because they cannot see what is no where to be seen.

I propose, in the following pages to give my lecture as already published, with remarks at the end upon the anonymous criticisms "published under the direction of the Temperance Society, Great Harwood."

PART III.

LECTURE.

IS TEETOTALISM THE PLAIN TEACHING OF THE OLD TESTAMENT?

THE question upon which we are now entering, is, in my opinion, a very important one; inasmuch as I deem the Word of God to be our principal authority in all matters pertaining to faith and practice. If the Bible forbids that I should eat anything, or drink anything, which in itself is represented as hurtful, then I am bound in obedience to the law of God, to refrain from that thing. I do not mean to say by this, that I feel myself bound by every precept of the Jewish *ceremonial* law, which was evidently designed for the regulation of the Jews as a nation. But this does not touch the matter in hand: for I cannot find in the ceremonial law any precept binding even upon the Jewish nation to abstain from strong drinks. The Jews were forbidden to *eat* many things that we eat; such as pork or the flesh of swine, hares, and all kinds of fish which are without fins and scales; different kinds of birds, and things that creep on the ground, were also forbidden; and, in *some circumstances*, wine and strong drink were forbidden; but the time during which the Israelites were to abstain, and the particular persons among them who were to abstain for that time which is mentioned, are distinctly specified.

But all this would be rather wonderful on the theory which a very few individuals wish to advocate, viz., that "TEETOTALISM," by which I suppose they mean *total abstinence*, "is the plain teaching of the Bible." What do they mean? Total abstinence always, and for every body, all the world over. How is it then that the law of Moses should specify only some particular times, and some particular individuals among the *Jewish* nation? And we know that the law of God, with respect to particular observances of eating and drinking, was stricter for the Jews than it was afterwards for the Christians; for we find Paul, under the Christian dispensation, speaking thus, in entire contradiction to the Jewish law: "I know, and am persuaded by the Lord Jesus, that there is nothing unclean of itself." That was a step in the direction of Christian liberty; and our Christian liberty (the New Testament tells us) is a thing which we are bound to hold sacred. Perhaps there are some—I am told of such—who would give Christians now less liberty than the Jews had. But we do not desire to put ourselves under their authority.

But as to the particular persons and times to which the prohibition of strong drinks was applicable, let me refer you to a few Scripture passages. The first is in Lev. x. 8, 9. We read there as follows:—" And the Lord spake unto Aaron, saying, Do not drink wine nor strong drink, thou, nor thy sons with thee, *when ye go into the tabernacle of the congregation*, lest ye die: it shall be a statute for ever throughout your generations." Let us again look at the law of the Nazarite. This is very clearly stated in Num. vi., from the first verse: " And the Lord spake unto Moses, saying, Speak unto the children of Israel, and say unto them, When either man or woman shall separate themselves to vow a vow of a Nazarite, to separate themselves unto the Lord; he shall separate himself from wine and strong drink, and shall drink no vinegar of wine, or vinegar of strong drink, neither shall he drink any liquor of grapes, nor eat moist grapes, or dried. All the days of his separation shall he eat nothing that is made of the vine tree, from the kernels even to the husk."—(1—4 verse.) But from the 13th verse we read concerning the law of the Nazarite, " when the days of his separation are fulfilled." There we are told that, at the time of his vow being accomplished, he should " be brought to the door of the tabernacle of the congregation," and that there he should offer his offering unto the Lord, and so on; and, after he had done all which the law required of him—so we read in the 20th verse—"*After that the Nazarite may drink wine.*" The word which is rendered *wine* in this place is the Hebrew *yayin;* and the signification which is given in Bagster's Hebrew Lexicon is "*wine,* or by metonymy," *i.e.* in which one word is sometimes put for another, as the cause for the effect, the same word is employed to denote "intoxication." In Eadie's Bible Cyclopædia we read of the Hebrew word *yayin,* which is here rendered wine as follows:—"Yayin was a generic name, and occurs a hundred and forty-one times in the Old Testament. In the majority of these instances it denotes a fermented and intoxicating liquid. It sometimes seems to signify the growing fruit of the vineyard, as in Deut. xxviii. 39; Jer. xl. 10—12. Such a use of the term is common in other wine countries. In Germany tho vinedresser will say in spring or summer—'the wine' blooms or flourishes well,—' the wine' will be good this season."

The same word *yayin* is used in both the cases to which I have been referring; both in the law pertaining to the priesthood, and in that of the Nazarites. You may say it was teetotal wine, if you please; but this very innocent wine called teetotal wine, which never intoxicates and which cannot intoxicate, which has never fermented and which does not contain a single particle of alcohol, I have never yet seen, nor have I heard what appears to me any very particular and authentic accounts concerning it. I confess that I have yet to learn that any such wine was ever in general and extensive use among the Hebrews, so as at all to warrant the application of the term *yayin* to it in particular. I may mention that upon this *yayin* Noah is said to have become drunken. Thus we read in Gen. ix. 21 : "And he drank of the wine *(yayin),* and was drunken." Upon this *yayin* too, of which, you will observe, it is positively said that the Nazarite might *drink* it, after the time of his vow was accomplished, the heart of King Ahasuerus is said to have become merry. Thus we read (Esth. i. 10, &c.): "On the seventh day, when the heart of the king was *merry with wine (yayin,* that is, in the original), he commanded his seven chamberlains to bring Vashti the queen before the king, to show the people and the princes her beauty; but the queen Vashti refused to como at the king's commandment." It was what some might call a drunken frolic on the part of Ahasuerus; and his wife, like a sensible woman, refused for once to obey the king's command.

In the passage which we heard about last Thursday evening, (Psalm lxxv. 8) * the same word is used, *yayin*, of which it is said the Nazarite might drink after his vow should be fulfilled. "For in the hand of the Lord there is a cup, and the wine (*yayin* again) is red." But I shall have something more to say presently about this passage and its context. In allusion to the exhilarating effects of this *yayin* it is said in Psalm lxxviii. 65, "Like a mighty man that shouteth by reason of wine." Here, again, it is the same word *yayin*. Look at Prov. xx. 1. "Wine is a mocker, strong drink is raging." We have the same word translated wine in this case: it is *yayin* that is said to mock or be a mocker. But was it said that the Nazarite, after he had fulfilled his vow, might drink that? Yes. Not, mark you, that he might be subject to mockery or insult; for in that case he would come under condemnation. You may have to do with a man that is a mocker; but you need not, if you have wisdom, be subject to his taunts, and derisions. There is no law in the word of God forbidding us to transact business, or to have ordinary dealings with a profane and wicked man. Nevertheless, it may, in some cases, be very dangerous and highly inexpedient to have to do with him. And in this passage where we are told that "wine is a mocker," we are put on our guard against it. It is not said, that we must never under any circumstances touch it; but it is said, "*Whosoever is deceived thereby is not wise*." Even to the Nazarite, after the fulfilment of his vow, it was said *you may drink wine*. But the same law which said that, said also, "if he bless himself in his heart, saying, I shall have peace, though I walk in the imagination of my heart, to add drunkenness to thirst: the Lord will not spare him, but then the anger of the Lord shall smoke against that man." Deut. xxix. 19, 20. "Wine is a mocker." Perhaps a man is a mocker. But this does not mean that either the man or the wine is *always* making a fool of people. All that can be said is, when you have to do with the one or the other, be on your proper guard, or you may be bitten to your hurt.

---

* Referred to by a Mr. Sandeman in the discussion, which followed a lecture delivered by me, on "True Temperance and the proper mode of advocating it."

To prove still more clearly that *yayin* had power to intoxicate, I will refer you to a few other passages. In Prov. xxiii. 29, 30, we read, "Who hath woe? Who hath sorrow? Who hath contentions? Who hath babbling? Who hath wounds without cause? Who hath redness of eyes? They that tarry long at the wine." *Yayin*, the word is here. The word which is rendered in the second clause of the 30th verse, "mixed wine," is another word entirely. But in the 31st verse, where we read, "Look not upon the wine when it is red," we have the term *yayin* repeated. But to this passage I shall return in another part of the Lecture. In Isaiah v. 11, we read, "Woe unto them that rise up early in the morning, that they may follow strong drink; that continue until night, till wine *(yayin)* inflame them." In Isaiah xxviii. 1, we read of "the head of the fat valleys of them that are *overcome with wine*" *(yayin)*. In the 7th verse of the same chapter, it is said, "They have erred through wine" *(yayin)*. In Jer. xxiii. 9, the prophet says, "Mine heart within me is broken because of the prophets; I am like a drunken man, and like a man whom wine *(yayin)* hath overcome."

But I think enough has been adduced to show that the *yayin* which the Nazarites were permitted to drink from the time that their vow had expired, was a beverage which might intoxicate. It is not necessary to prove that the term was never employed to denote the unfermented fruit of the grape. It might have been so employed sometimes. But it is altogether *inadmissible* to suppose that, in the case of the Nazarite who had fulfilled his vow, the term must be taken to signify *only that which did not intoxicate*. No doubt the permission was given to use that which the term *yayin* most generally denoted; and it is plain to any impartial mind which will be at the trouble to investigate the matter, that that was a drink which might intoxicate, and did intoxicate when taken to excess.

But you may remember that the priests were forbidden to drink either *wine* or *strong drink* when they went into the tabernacle of the congregation; and that the Nazarite, during the time of his vow, was to "separate himself from *wine* and *strong drink*." You will observe that *two* kinds of drink are mentioned: and from the prohibition to use these at the particular times which are specified we might reasonably conclude that the prohibition did not hold good at other times. When the Israelites were forbidden to eat the flesh of swine, no particular time was mentioned; but the command was intended to hold good continually. "Of their flesh shall ye not eat, and their carcase shall ye not touch; they are unclean to you."—Lev. xi. 8. Such was the Jewish law with regard to swine. Of course that was for the Jewish nation only. Gentiles under the Christian dispensation are exempt from the Jewish ceremonial law. But not even does the ceremonial law of the Jews anywhere forbid the use of wine and strong drink, except in the case of the Nazarite, and the priests when entering into the temple.

We have seen that in the case of the Nazarite, the permission was given to drink the *yayin* or wine after the time of his vow was accomplished, and this *yayin*, we have seen, was of an intoxicating nature. But in the law of Moses, permission was given, not only to make use of the *yayin*, but also to use the *shechar* or *strong drink*. If you look at Deut. xiv., you will find towards the end of the chapter an account of the law pertaining to the Jewish tithe. The tenth part of all the produce of the fields, and vineyards, and herds, and flocks, belonging to the Israelites, was said to be holy unto the Lord. God had appointed that this should be given to the children of Levi, who were ordained, as ministers of religion, to the service of the tabernacle. And the law in this chapter, from the 22nd verse, is as follows: "Thou shalt truly tithe all the increase of thy seed, that the field bringeth forth year by year. And thou shalt eat before the Lord thy God, in the place which He shall choose to place His name there, the tithe of thy corn, of thy wine, and of thine oil, and the firstlings of thy herds and of thy flocks." Here I would wish you to observe, please, that the word which is translated wine is not *yayin* but *tirosh*, the signification of which is given in the Hebrew Lexicons as *new wine* or *must*, although Gesenius says, I know, that this word sometimes denoted a certain kind of wine which had intoxicating qualities. "The term *tirosh*," says Dr. Eadie, "appears often to mean the solid produce of the vine, and is frequently used along with the word *corn*, or field produce, and *oil*, or orchard produce.

But let us go on to the following verses. The Israelites were told in these, that if the way from their respective homes to the place of the Lord's house, which, as you will remember, was afterward at Jerusalem: if the way were too long to admit of their carrying the produce of their field, vineyards, &c.; then they were to turn it all into money. They were to sell their tithe offering, and bind up the money in their hand, and go unto the place which God would choose. "And," so we read the law in the 26th and 27th verses, "thou shalt bestow that money for whatsoever thy soul lusteth after, for oxen, or for sheep, or for wine, or for strong drink, or for whatsoever thy soul desireth; and thou shalt eat there before the Lord thy God." The words which are here rendered *wine* and *strong drink* are *yayin* and *shechar*. Observe, then, the law is given that the Israelites might, if they saw fit, sell their *tirosh*, which, according to the meaning which is given, was a sort of new wine or must: they might sell that, and turn it into money; and with the money they might buy *yayin*, or wine, and *shechar*, or strong intoxicating drink; not that they might get drunk upon it, for drunkenness was strictly forbidden; but the commandment said: "And thou shalt eat (or make use of) it there before the Lord thy God, and thou shalt rejoice, thou, and thine household, and the Levite that is within thy gates; thou shalt not forsake him; for he hath no part nor inheritance with thee." The Levites had no possession in lands or flocks as the other Israelites had; and therefore they were to be cared for by all the tribes.

Let me now say a little about this other word which has been mentioned, *shechar*. The priests were not to touch this *shechar*, or the *yayin* when they went into the house of the Lord. Why? Evidently, because it had power to intoxicate if taken in considerable quantities. If this were not the reason, what other can be assigned?. It would not be seemly that the priests should be at all exposed to the danger of drunkenness when going to minister in the sanctuary. Therefore, as it seems to me, they were not then to take any kind of wine or strong drink. The only definitions which Bagster's Hebrew Lexicon gives me of the term *shechar* is this: "Strong intoxicating drink." Such is the signification given by Gesenius. Another Hebrew Lexicon gives the following:

"*potus inebrians, temetum, sicera;*" i.e., intoxicating drink, strong wine, all manner of strong drink. I may add that I have looked, so far as I know, into every case where the word "strong drink" is used in our English Bible; and in each case I find the word thus rendered to be the same Hebrew word, *shechar*.

I do not think that I can do better, in giving the full signification of *shechar*, than to quote what Dr. Eadie says about it in his Bible Cyclopædia:—

"*Drink, Strong.*—The Hebrew term *shechar*, rendered "strong drink," is, according to the highest of living authorities, Dr. Julius Fürst, of Leipzig, from an etymon, which is found in Sanscrit, and common to many languages. The root is *ker*, and is seen in the Latin *cremare*. The term, denoting "strong drink," from a root signifying *to burn*, may refer either to the mode of preparing it, or to the burning and feverish effects of intoxication. Others suppose it to be allied to a large family of words found in almost all tongues; shechar being a sister term to sugar, suckar in Scotch, zucker in German, saccharum in Latin, with other similar forms existing in many of the oriental vocabularies. The root is often used in Scripture to denote intoxication, as Gen. ix. 21; 1 Sam. i. 13, 25—36; 2 Sam. xi. 13; 1 Kings xx. 16; Job xii. 25; Psalm cvii. 27; Isaiah xix. 14; Jer. xxiii. 9. In all these passages, the verb or its participle refers to intoxication; as they refer to Noah, who was so drunk, that he lay shamelessly without apparel; to Hannah, who appeared to Eli to mutter unintelligibly under stupifying inebriation; to Nabal, who was sunk into utter insensibility, and to the staggering and vomiting which strong drink produces. The noun which claims kindred with such a verb, and which differs from it only very slightly in pronounciation, is naturally supposed to signify a variety of intoxicating drinks. The prophet Isaiah describes it as producing the same sensual and beastly effects as wine. 'But they also have erred through wine, and through strong drink are out of the way; the priest and the prophet have erred through strong drink, they are swallowed up of wine, they are out of the way through strong drink; they err in vision, they stumble in judgment. For all tables are full of vomit and filthiness, so that there is no place clean.'" (Isaiah xxviii., 7 and 8 vs.)

"The term, therefore, seems to indicate any intoxicating drink, whether brewed from grain or made of honeycombs, dates, or boiled fruits. The Alexandrian interpreters, who were doubtless familiar with the barley-wine or beer of Egypt, render this word by other terms signifying intoxicating drink. Jerome, who in this case 'spake what he knew,' says that shechar means every sort of drink that can intoxicate, which is made from grain or apple-juice, or when honey-combs are boiled down into a sweet and barbarous beverage, or the fruit of the palm squeezed out and made into liquor, and when water receives a colour and consistency from prepared herbs. The phrase, 'wine and strong drink,' occurs together several times in Scripture, probably one-and-twenty times, and plainly means wine and every other intoxicating liquor. Thus the Chaldee paraphrasts understood it, so did Philo the Jew, for the explanation we have given is just his definition, as well as that of Origen the great biblical scholar of early times. Shechar is 'stupefying,' says Chrysostom, and Jerome often translates the term by the simple word *ebrietas*, drunkenness. Hesychius defines it as meaning intoxicating drink, not made from grapes. With the Hebrews, says Suidas, this name is given to an intoxicating liquor —spiced wine. The priests when about to officiate, and the Nazarite during his vow, were to drink neither wine nor strong drink—neither wine nor any other intoxicating draught. When Hannah justified herself from the imputation of Eli, she said, 'I have drunk neither wine, nor strong drink,' neither wine, nor any other intoxicating beverage. .' Wine is a mocker, strong drink is raging.' The cognate Arabic terms also denote drunkenness. Maimonides, the famous rabbi, says, that 'strong drink' is made from crushed wheat, barley, and other. things. In some passages of Scripture, the allied verb does not describe absolute intoxication, yet it seems to imply the use of the liquor which if taken to excess, possessed the power of inebriating. That the Hebrews had sweet *shrubs*, syrups or *dibs*, no one will deny; but none of these ever come under the designation of 'strong drink' in Scripture. 'Strong drink' is not sweet drink, nor can a mere figure, as in Isaiah xxiv. 9, prove it; and shechar surely can at no time mean the mere fruit of he palm, any more than *ale* can signify the barley from which it is brewed—barley either in its natural or malted state. In Numbers vi. 3, Onkelos renders the term by 'old wine.' If we compare Exod. xxviii. 7, we shall find that strong drink is used in the latter passage for wine itself. And lastly, Bishop Lowth, though he maintains that 'sweet drink' is the correct rendering of shechar, says, on Isaiah v. 11, that it has 'its name from its remarkable *inebriating* qualities.'

"Other nations had the same beverage. Pliny enumerates various vegetables which enter into his composition: among the rest, figs, pomegranates, apples, and particularly dates. This date wine was in great request among the Parthians, Indians, and other Orientals; and is said by Xenophon to produce severe headaches. We may naturally infer that the strong drink includes this liquor of dates, as well as other artificial beverages."

Before I go further, I would wish to lay down in very few words what I conceive to be the teaching of the Bible respecting wines and strong drinks, or any kinds of drink which have power to intoxicate. I do not believe, and after what I have shown to night you would generally think it strange if I did—I do not believe that the Bible teaches total abstinence for all persons for all times. It does nothing of the kind. But this it does: it pronounces many severe judgments on those who err through an excessive indulgence in strong drink; and in some cases, on the other hand, it tells us that those who refrained from it altogether partook of the Divine blessing, and God's favour was manifest towards them. I may refer in proof of this latter statement to the fact that the sons of Jonadab, the son of Rechab, were approved of God on account of their obedience to their father Jonadab: and Daniel, whom we know to have been an abstainer, at least for some considerable portion of his life, was a man greatly owned, and beloved, and blessed of God. But these cases of what might be denominated "total abstinence," with a very few others, such as that of the companions of Daniel, Hananiah, Mishael, and Azariah, who abstained with him, were exceptional cases. The Jews were not at any time a nation of teetotallers. Certainly there can be no evidence to prove that they were; or that they violated the law and commandment of God in making merely a moderate use of strong drink. We know very well that in different ages many of the Jews, and among them priests and prophets, and princes, were addicted to the shameful sin of drunkenness, and they are condemned, not because they were not teetotallers, but because they were drunken. "The priest and the prophet," said Isaiah, xxviii. 7, 8, "have erred through strong drink, they are swallowed up of wine, they are out of the way through strong drink; they err in vision, they stumble in judgment. For all tables are full of vomit, and filthiness, so that there is no place clean." And as we think of these excesses on the part of God's professed ministers, we cannot wonder that the Divine wrath should have been kindled against them.

But it may be asked, were not all the *good* people among the Israelites abstainers? The fact is, there were *none perfect*. The best of the Old Testament saints were sinful men, and had need to look up to the pardoning mercy of God as much as any of us. But with the exception of Daniel, and his companions, and perhaps Samuel the prophet, we do not know of any abstainers, who were particularly distinguished in the Old Testament for their goodness. Sampson was a Nazarite, at least up to the time when he suffered his wife to betray him, and the hair of his head was shorn, and then it is intimated the Lord departed from him. Sampson was a very strong man; but as to the moral excellence of his character, I do not know that we can say very much for that. The Israelites, while they were in the wilderness on their way from Egypt to Canaan were certainly abstainers, so far as the *yayin*, and *shechar*, and *bread* were concerned. Thus we read the words of the Lord to the Israelites in Deut. xxix. 5, 6, as follows—"And I have led you forty years in the wilderness; your clothes are not waxen old upon you, and thy shoe is not waxen old upon thy foot. *Ye have not eaten bread, neither have ye drunk wine or strong drink: that ye might know that I am the Lord your God.*" But the Israelites in the wilderness were not much the better for being abstainers: for, with two exceptions, all were destroyed before they took possession of the promised land; and that, for their sins and transgressions, and rebellion against God; Joshua and Caleb being the only two individuals who came out of Egypt that were permitted to enter the promised inheritance. We know that when Melchizedek, king of Salem, met Abram, as he was returning from the pursuit of those who had stolen his nephew Lot, and his goods, Melchizedek brought forth bread and wine *(yayin)*, and it is highly probable that Abram partook of his hospitality. If so, neither Melchizedek nor Abram would appear to be total abstainers. But Melchizedek is spoken of in the New Testament as a *king of righteousness*, which, according to the Hebrew idiom, is equivalent to saying that he was a *righteous king;* and we are also told that he was "priest of the most high God." Abram was noted for his fidelity; and was certainly one of the most eminent among the Old Testament saints and patriarchs. It was said of Noah before the flood that he was "a just man and upright in his generations," though it is a sufficient proof that he was not absolutely perfect, that he afterwards fell through the sin of drunkenness. Noah, therefore, was not an abstainer.

I have said that in some cases those who refrained from wine partook of the Divine blessing. But we cannot say that God blessed them merely because they were abstainers from wine. The sons of Jonadab, the sons of Rechab, were blessed *because they obeyed the command of their father* Jonadab. Jeremiah was told to go to the house of the Rechabites, "and give them wine *(yayin)* to drink; and if you read Jer. xxxv. ch., from 5th v., you will find the words of the prophet as follows:—" And I set before the sons of the house of the Rechabites pots full of wine *(yayin)*, and cups, and I said unto them—'Drink ye wine.'" From this it does not appear probable that Jeremiah himself was an abstainer. "But they said, we will drink no wine; for Jonadab the son of Rechab our father commanded us, saying, Ye shall drink no wine, neither ye, nor your sons for ever: neither shall ye build house, nor sow seed, nor plant vineyard, nor have any; but all your days ye shall dwell in tents; that ye may live many days in the land where ye be strangers. Thus, said they, have we obeyed the voice of Jonadab, the son of Rechab, our father, in all that he hath charged us, to drink no wine all our days, we, our wives, our sons, nor our daughters; nor to build houses for us to dwell in; neither have we vineyard, nor field, nor seed; but we have dwelt in tents, and have obeyed, and done according to all that Jonadab our father commanded us."

Now for the lesson, or argument, which is to be drawn from this. Jeremiah was commanded to go and tell the men of Judah, and the inhabitants of Jerusalem, how that the sons of Jonadab had obeyed the voice of their earthly father; and to contrast with their filial obedience the *disobedience of them who refused to acknowledge the authority of a Heavenly father*. The argument based on the conduct of the sons of Jonadab is, not that all men ought, therefore, to abstain from wine, and dwell in tents, and refuse to build houses, and to give up sowing seed and planting vineyards, as the Rechabites did: but it is similar to what we find in Malachi, where we read the words of the Lord to the priests of the house of Israel thus—"A son honoureth his father, and a servant his master; if then I be a father, where is mine honour? and if I be a master, where is my fear?" Mal. i. 6. "Then," we read, "came the word of the Lord unto Jeremiah, saying, Thus saith the Lord of hosts, the God of Israel; Go and tell the men of Judah, and the inhabitants of Jerusalem, Will ye not receive instruction to hearken to my words? saith the Lord. The words of Jonadab, the son of Rechab, that he commanded his sons not to drink wine, are performed; for unto this day they drink none, but obey their father's commandment. Notwithstanding I have spoken unto you, rising early and speaking; but ye hearkened not unto me. I have sent also unto you all my servants the prophets, rising up early and sending them, saying, Return ye now every man from his evil way, and amend your doings, and go not after other gods to serve them, and ye shall dwell in the land which I have given to you and to your fathers; but ye have not inclined your ear, nor hearkened unto me. Because the sons of Jonadab, the son of Rechab, have performed the commandment of their father, which he commanded them; but this people hath not hearkened unto me; therefore, thus saith the Lord God of hosts, the God of Israel; Behold, I will bring upon Judah, and upon all the inhabitants of Jerusalem, all the evil that I have pronounced against them; because I have spoken unto them, but they have not heard; and I have called unto them, but they have not answered." Jer. xxxv., 12—17.

With respect to the case of Daniel we cannot say that it was *because he abstained from wine* that God blessed him. A vegetarian might say that it was because he refused to eat animal food, and preferred to live upon pulse. Another who condemns the use of tea and coffee, as well as flesh, might say Daniel was blessed because he lived on pulse and water. My own theory is that Daniel was blessed of God because he set his heart to seek God and to keep his commandments, trusting only in the mercy of God for salvation.

Teetotalism may be properly regarded, I think, as in entire harmony with the teaching of God's word. But it is not *therefore* to be considered as binding upon all men. It may be in perfect accordance with the teachings of the Bible that we live in a certain town or village, and that we are engaged there in a particular calling. Are all persons therefore required to live where we live, and to do as we do? A certain kind of diet may be agreeable and necessary for one; and it may be said that it is quite in harmony, or in accordance with the law of the Bible, that such a diet should be made use of. Is every person obliged therefore to eat and drink the same, and in the same way? It is one thing to say that teetotalism is in harmony with the Bible; but it is altogether different to say that it is "the plain teaching of the Bible." If teetotalism be so plainly taught in the Scriptures, as some profess to believe it is, then I must confess that I am exceedingly dull in apprehending the truth, and should employ some one else to see for me. I have been looking long for this said teetotalism as the plain teaching of the Bible; and I cannot help thinking that those who can find it there, have a magnifying glass of such power as I cannot boast of; and to say the truth, I think I would rather do without it; for strong magnifiers are hurtful for weak eyes.

But I have promised to return to one or two passages which perhaps claim an additional notice, inasmuch as they have been pleaded on a former occasion in evidence of the scriptural teaching of total abstinence. The former of these is in Psalm lxxv. 8: "For in the hand of the Lord there is a cup, and the wine is red; it is full of mixture: and he poureth out of the same; but the dregs thereof, all the wicked of the earth shall wring them out, and drink them." It has been said that this passage is one which proves that we should not have anything to do with intoxicating drinks, because this red wine is a symbol of the divine anger. But it would seem to be an unfortunate fact in the way of our accepting this theory, that the most of what are called teetotal wines are of a red colour. Gin and whiskey are *not* red; neither is pale bitter ale red. It so happens that I have seen some rigid teetotallers drink wine, which has precisely answered the description in this text. It has been red, and thick, as if it were filled with some kind of mixture ; and after the liquor has been drunk, I have noticed a sediment in the glass; and of all the persons in the world, the teetotaller has been the one to drink the very dregs of this cup, or glass of—very innocent teetotal wine.

Did it never occur to the gentleman who adduced this passage to prove that the Bible teaches teetotalism, * that a symbol may have two very different and even opposite meanings ? If we take the expression *red wine,* we find it in our English version in two very different connections. Undoubtedly, it was sometimes symbolical of the wrath of God. But turn to Isaiah xxvii. 2, 3; and you will there read as follows, where the reference is evidently to the *Church of God:* "Sing ye unto her, a vineyard of *red wine.* I the Lord do keep it; I will water it every moment : lest any hurt it, I will keep it night and day." If we consider the cup, there can be no doubt that when the Psalmist speaks in Psalm cxvi. 13, of the "*cup of salvation,*" the symbol must be regarded as one of blessing, not of the Divine anger; although the figure in the Psalmist's mind was probably very similar to that which is described in Psalm lxxv. 8. In xxiii. 5, the Psalmist says in view of the Divine mercies : " Thou preparest a table before me in the presence of mine enemies : Thou anointest my head with oil ; *my cup* runneth over." Here again I take the liberty to think that David had in view the cup of wine which was usually present at a

---

* The Gentleman here referred to is Mr. Sandeman, of Church. It may be necessary to mention, that, as he had opposed some statements which I had made in a preceding lecture, I thought it proper to refer here to his argument ; not as the Author of the Reply wishes to make it appear, to Dr. Lees. No allusion was made in this Lecture either to Dr. Lees, or to any thing which I knew him to have said.

feast. Take the emblem of fire. Allusion is made by it to the fire of Divine love, of holy charity, or of religious meditation. "While I was musing," said the Psalmist, "the fire burned." But no doubt, fire sometimes, like thunder, and lightning, and the dregs of a bitter cup, must be regarded as the symbol of vengeance. Are we then to say that fire is a bad thing? No: it is a good thing if we make a good use of it. The cup of blessing will be good, if we make a wise and good use of it; otherwise the blessing itself may be turned into a curse.

It is rather the *dregs* in this cup of the 75th Psalm, that must be considered as symbolizing the essence of the curse. Take the context in the 7th verse, with what follows. The Psalmist there speaks of God as a discriminating judge. "He putteth down one," we read, "and setteth up another." All are not dealt with alike; but every man is rewarded according to his deeds. "For," says the Psalmist, " in the hand of the Lord there is a cup, and the wine is red ; it is full of mixture." Allusion is here made to the practice of flavouring and increasing the strength of wines. "And He poureth out of the same." That is, as it appears to me, that all might drink it, with its good or evil, or whatever it might be ; whether blessing, or affliction and sorrow and woe. "But," said the Psalmist, "the dregs thereof, (that is the worst of it) all the wicked of the earth shall wring them out, and drink them."*

In Isaiah li. 17; 22, we have a repetition of the symbol which is here employed ; and you may observe that there also the emphasis seems to be laid on "the *dregs of the cup*." Thus we read the prophetic call: "Stand up, O Jerusalem, which hast drunk at the hand of the Lord the cup of His fury; thou hast drunken the *dregs* of the cup of trembling, and wrung them out." "Thus saith the Lord, behold, I have taken out of thy hand the cup of trembling,

---

* Scott, in his commentary on this passage, makes, I think, some very judicious and excellent remarks. "Heavenly blessings," he says, "are in Scripture represented by a cup of wholesome, exhilarating wine; but the wrath of God is represented by a cup of wine mingled with ingredients of that kind which tend to produce fear, distress, and despondency ; and, if drunk to excess, horror, infatuation, anguish, and despair. From this cup the Lord dispenses as he pleaseth to sinners in this world ; and even His people drink some of the wine contained in it, when chastened in his fatherly displeasure ; but the dregs of it will be the portion of the impenitent hereafter, who will wring them out and drink them all to eternity."

even the *dregs* of the cup of my fury; thou shalt no more drink it again."

With respect to the peculiar power of *red wine* more than any other wine to intoxicate, I am altogether in the dark. *Yayin* is the word here used; and *yayin*, we know, was generally a wine which would intoxicate. Whether red wine, or yellow wine, or wine of any other colour was *most* intoxicating among the ancient Hebrews, I believe it would puzzle all the learned men in Europe to decide. But some persons near at hand may tell us all about it, perhaps, if we will take their word for it. The red colour was no doubt symbolical of vengeance; probably for this reason, that it was the colour of blood. Thus the garments of the Redeemer were said in Isa. lxiii. to be stained with red; for He said: "I have trodden the winepress alone; and of the people there was none with me: for I will tread them in mine anger, and trample them in my fury; and their *blood* shall be sprinkled upon my garments, and I will stain all my raiment." And thus we read of the sword of the Almighty, when He takes vengeance on His enemies, as being red with blood. But we must not suppose, that, therefore, blood is in itself a bad thing. It would be a sign of very great weakness for a man to jump at such a conclusion as that. Both red wine and red blood may be regarded sometimes as the symbol of wrath; and yet in themselves they may be both very good.

But in opposition to the statement, that this wine or *yayin*, that had an intoxicating property, was to be regarded as an unholy thing; let me remind you that this very *yayin* was to be offered in the Jewish temple as a holy offering with the morning and evening sacrifice. If you look at Exod. xxix. 39, 40, you will read as follows: "The one lamb thou shalt offer in the morning; and the other lamb thou shalt offer at even: and with the one lamb a tenth deal of flour mingled with the fourth part of a hin of beaten oil; and the fourth part of a hin (or about two and a half pints) of wine (*yayin)* for a drink offering." And it is further commanded that the priests should do to the lamb which was to be offered for the evening sacrifice "according to the meat offering of the morning, and according to the drink offering thereof." The priests were not to *drink* the *yayin* when they went into the holy place: nevertheless it was *consecrated* in being offered unto God as a drink offering. Wherefore my advice is that we call not this *yayin* an evil thing, though the abuse of it was doubtless wicked and inexpedient.

Let me observe again, that this *yayin* is referred to in the Scriptures as the *symbol of gospel blessings; e.g.* in Isa. lv. 1: where we read: " Ho, every one that thirsteth, come ye to the waters, and he that hath no money; come ye, buy and eat; yea, come, buy wine (*yayin*) and milk without money and without price." But *yayin* was intoxicating, was it not? Yes. And yet it was the symbol of gospel blessings? Yes. Then what becomes of the argument, that because it was the symbol of vengeance, we must regard it as in itself an accursed thing? A peculiar kind of red wine, drugged, and having a peculiar power to stupify, and to fill the mind with dread and astonishment, might have been to the Jews an apt symbol of wrath. But that same wine, when taken in a proper manner, and in reasonable quantity, might have exhilarated and cheered the heart. Such wine may be abused now, so as to produce drunkenness; and it may be very proper for us generally to abstain from it. Nevertheless, it must be numbered among the gifts of God; and should be regarded as having a beneficial design in connection with its bestowment.

We may select one other instance, in which wine must evidently be taken as the symbol of what is good; and in this case again it is the *yayin* which is spoken of. Turn to Prov. ix. 1, 2, where we read: " Wisdom hath builded her house, she hath hewn out her seven pillars; she hath killed her beasts; she hath mingled her wine *(yayin)*; she hath also furnished her table." It is plainly the wisdom of God which is here spoken of. And in the following verses we read: " As for him that wanteth understanding, she saith to him, come, eat of my bread. and drink of the *wine which I have mingled.*" If we consider then the place which the *yayin*, and even the mixed *yayin* or wine, maintains in the *symbology* of the Old Testament, we shall find that it is not to be despised on that account.

One other passage demands a brief consideration: Prov. xxiii. 31. " Look not thou upon the wine when it is red, when it giveth his colour in the cup, when it moveth itself aright." What the moving itself aright may mean in this passage I am not careful to learn. A total abstainer may think that the wine moves itself aright, when it is put over the fire, and got up to boiling heat, and he might expect the alcohol to go up the chimney. But whatever mode of interpretation be adopted, this passage cannot be taken as a Scriptural command to avoid the use of all intoxicating drinks: for many of these do not move, nor sparkle in the cup, nor are they red. Much that passes under the name of *teetotal* beverage answers as much to the description which is here conveyed, as some alcoholic drinks. If I mistake not, I have seen some coloured effervescing draughts, which are considered innocuous by abstainers, but which might be productive, nevertheless, of serious consequences if taken to excess.

But the injunction in the passage under consideration says—*Look not.* Does that mean, *thou shalt not taste?* If so, we can well understand what swallowing a camel may mean to those who have ever *seen* one. But if the command, *look not,* does not mean, *thou shalt not taste or swallow,* then perhaps it means really what it says and no more. In that case, those who love to load themselves with disabilities, may add to the list—*touch not, taste not, handle not,* this other, *look not.* Will they then go through the world with their eyes bandaged? But I really hope that our *very* abstinent friends will not so far despise the use of their eyes as to rob themselves of the luxury of sight. The command is intelligible enough to any one who does not want to make more of the text than is intended by it. Take the expression, *look not,* for what it is worth in other passages; *e. g.* 2 Cor. iv. 18: "While we *look* not at the things which are seen, but at the things which are not seen." Again, Phil. ii. 4: "*Look not* every man on his own things, but every man also on the things of others." Will any one say that the meaning of the expression "*look not,*" in these passages is simply "*taste not?*" Does it not rather signify that we are not to look upon those things which are referred to *with inordinate desire and affection?* Precisely so in the case coming before us in the Proverbs. Solomon seems to have written specially for the benefit of young men who were in danger of being ensnared through habits of profligacy. He bade them, therefore, to beware, especially at their feasts, of setting their eyes and their desires too much upon the intoxicating draught. In the beginning of the same chapter he had used language just as strong, or even stronger, about the necessity of guarding the appetite, when seated at the ruler's table. "When thou sittest to eat with a ruler," said the wise man, "consider diligently what is before thee; and put a knife to thy throat, if thou be a man given to appetite. Be not desirous of his dainties, for they are *deceitful meat*." King Solomon might have said concerning those edible luxuries with which the ruler's table was spread, as well as of the deceitful *wine*—" At the last it biteth like a serpent, and stingeth like an adder." Of course it would do so, if taken in too great abundance; for deceitful meat, or dainties of any kind, are dangerous for weak souls.

In conclusion, I would say that, to those who are not void of understanding, the Bible teaches very plainly what is the whole duty of man. But above all, it teaches us to put our trust in God. It tells us that " he that trusteth in his own heart is a fool;" " but he that trusteth in the Lord, mercy shall compass him about." As for opposing teetotalism, I should never dream of it. I believe that it is our bounden duty as Christians to be as frugal and temperate as possible; and teetotalism with those who are in health, I believe to be nothing less, in general, than a wise method of economising health and money. But I cannot conceal from myself or others the conviction, that stimulating drinks are given with a wise design by an all-wise and merciful Benefactor; and though they have been most fearfully abused, even to the ruin of thousands and tens of thousands of the human race, it will do no good to prop up the cause of temperance by misrepresentation. God helping me, I will speak the truth, so far as I know it; and I am content to leave the results in the hands of Him who is the God of truth.

May He in mercy lead the world to see that it is not *one* particular form of temperance alone, which is the world's bane and curse; but SIN as *sin*, originated and maintained by forgetfulness of God, and contempt of His authority.

PART IV.

REMARKS ON THE REPLY.

Much shallow disputation, in reply to the foregoing lecture, proceeds on the wrong assumption that I have there taken notice of some statements, or modes of argument employed by Dr. Lees. It may serve to remove misapprehension to affirm what I have declared before, that my lecture contains not the slightest reference to any thing which the Doctor has ever said or written, excepting, perhaps, this one proposition which appeared in the announcement of a lecture to be delivered by Dr. Lees: "Teetotalism the plain teaching of the Bible." I have, therefore, neither represented nor misrepresented him. I had no more idea that the Doctor had treated the people of Harwood to a lecture which was already in print than I had of his giving them the Queen's speech which had been last delivered to her Lords and Commons in Parliament. If I had been aware that I could purchase what he had said, before giving my lecture, I might have endeavoured to follow him in his argument. But, perhaps, it was as well that I went at once to the Bible; for, certainly, as we would know what the Bible plainly teaches, the book to be examined is the Bible; and to say that we cannot understand what the Bible teaches without asking Dr. Lees is not only an insult to our common understanding, but it is at the same time to give up the point of "the plain teaching of the Bible" altogether.

One might have supposed, until we are informed to the contrary, that my friend, Mr. Wilkinson, and I, at least understood the subject to be discussed. But, according to our Critic, we did not. Let us take the first words of his very brilliant reply.

"The author of the first pamphlet, published many years ago, (named a lecture on the Harmony of Teetotalism with the Divine Word) having recently delivered it as a lecture, under the title of 'Teetotalism the plain teaching of Scripture,' Messrs. Wilkinson and Williams, it seems, have taken umbrage at the assertion."

No umbrage at all, my dear Sir. Umbrage means, I suppose, a shade or shadow. But neither were our intellects nor our hearts shadowed by such a statement. Messrs. Wilkinson and Williams enjoyed a hearty laugh at the matter, and wondered what new light would come next.

"And without either hearing, or apparently reading, the matured lecture of Dr. Lees, have rushed into ineraseable print."

As I have observed before, I could not hear the Doctor's lecture, neither could Mr. Wilkinson hear it, for we both had engagements of another kind to attend to on the evening of its delivery; and who would have thought of sending for a printed "Lecture on the Harmony of Teetotalism with the Divine Word," to discover what Dr. Lees had said at a public meeting to prove Teetotalism to be "the plain teaching of the Bible." But our Critic displays a surprising facility in veering from one point to another. Here he has it: "*Without either hearing*, or apparently reading, the lecture of Dr. Lees." And after this he goes on to lavish almost every species of abuse because I have not fairly represented Dr. Lees. I had something else to do than to represent Dr. Lees: my duty was to enquire, without bias and without partiality, what is "the plain teaching of the Bible."

The Replier complains of

"The puerile distinction" "between the Bible *teaching* Teetotalism, and the Bible *harmonising* with it! which shows," he says, "as great an ignorance of the meaning of words as of the conditions of reasoning."

Indeed! Then the Replier really supposes that a book can never harmonize with anything which is not contained in the book itself! Harmony, according to the passage now quoted, signifies, not concord or agreement, but sameness. And hence our Critic may go on to affirm that, as the statements and representations of the Bible harmonize with all the known principles of Astronomy, the Bible teaches those Astronomical principles, or if the Bible record concerning the formation of the earth harmonize with the clearest deductions of Geology, then the Bible teaches plainly all that we know about it. I thankfully accept the sensible verdict, quoted, on the title page of our Critic's Reply, from the Duke of Argyle. His language as there given is as follows: "*I have no intention of entering upon the religious difficulties which the progress of geological discoveries has been supposed to raise. A large number of them have been overcome: that is to say, they have been seen to be no real difficulties at all, but to have depended, as in the case of Astronomy, on the erroneous principles of interpretation which had been applied to the words of Scripture.*" Here the quotation ends: but the Author of the Reply is not content with that: he therefore seeks to add point to it by affixing something of his own which follows in brackets. Thus the public are made to read as follows: "—'which had been applied to the words of Scripture' (by its professed expounders)." This is rather an equivocal compliment to Dr. Lees; for if he is not a professed expounder of Scripture, who is? But will the Duke of Argyle sanction the statement that because Astronomy, and Geology, and Teetotalism, are in harmony with the Word of God, therefore they are all plainly taught in that Word? I trow not. The author of the Reply knew from my published lecture that Teetotalism had raised no difficulties in my mind as to the harmonizing of its general practice with the teachings of the Bible. It is the irrelevant conclusion, jumped at by Dr. Lees, that, therefore, Teetotalism is the plain teaching of the Bible, that I demur to: and, I suppose, his Grace the Duke of Argyle would smile at this freak of our Teetotal Doctor as much as any other man who has common understanding.

To extend our quotation a little, let us take the following :

"Teetotalism is abstinence from toxic-drink, and the discountenancing of *all* drinking customs, on the ground that Alcohol is a bad article, not 'a good creature.' If the Bible plainly teaches that such drink is bad, then it harmonizes with Teetotalism; if it teaches that intoxicating drink is good, then it contradicts Teetotalism."

For myself, I cannot accept the definition of Teetotalism, here quoted, as any definition at all. What *kind* of abstinence is required? Total abstinence always, in health or sickness? Abstinence from what is designated "toxic-drink," whether as a beverage, or a medicine? The writer should have explained himself so as to be understood. Then there are various kinds of "toxic-drink" besides what are alcoholic. But drinks which might be more or less toxical, or poisonous, to persons in perfect health, may be properly employed for the mitigation of extreme suffering. Teetotalism is further said to be "the discountenancing of *all* drinking customs," and "*all*" is rendered by the Replier emphatic. What is this but sheer nonsense in the way of definition? Our Critic may affect to despise the limits assigned by the common use of words: but if he chooses to attempt a definition in words, he should content himself with being simply definite, intelligible, and correct. What, I would ask, is the common practice of drinking water, or milk, or tea, but a drinking custom? Is it not as much so as the drinking of wine, or ale, or spirituous liquors? I am thankful to believe that the former kind of drinking is much more customary than the latter. But, according to our Critic's definition of Teetotalism, we are seriously required to discountenance "*all* drinking customs." Query: will it be rational to give up the custom of drinking at breakfast and at tea time?

As for the declaration, "that alcohol is a bad article"; that is no more the language of Science than it is of Revelation. Certainly, the Bible does not teach that alcohol is bad, for it nowhere says anything about alcohol, although it says much about wine, and strong drink, in which, it is evident, a greater or less amount of alcohol was present; but neither is the alcohol, nor the drink which contained it, specially denounced as a bad article any more than meat or drink in general. But any man of ordinary judgment may see that it is not necessary for the Bible to contradict the plain teachings of science, by affirming that alcohol is in itself a bad article, before it can be said to harmonize with the principles of a legitimate Teetotalism. The Bible neither affirms, nor denies, anything about the goodness of alcohol. But it would be singular presumption for any man to say that, therefore, the conduct of a Teetotaller in abstaining does not harmonize with the Word of God.

But to continue our quotation from the point where we left off :—

"The opponents are very elaborately emphatic about some fancied difference between the Bible *teaching* Teetotalism, and the Bible *harmonizing* with it ! which shows as great an ignorance of the meaning of words as of the conditions of reasoning. The puerile distinction is the more inexcusable, since Dr. Lees distinctly explains the sense of his proposition :—'The Teetotallers do *not* seek to base their doctrines *upon* the Bible, but are satisfied to affirm their harmony with it'.........'Where do you find a single text that, clearly and explicitly, represents God as contradicting these doctrines ?' "

I believe that Dr. Lees is quite right when he represents that the Teetotallers are generally much too sensible to think of basing their doctrines upon the Bible, and that they, like myself, " are satisfied to affirm their harmony with it." I hope too that, by this time, even Dr. Lees begins to see that it is much safer to rest satisfied with the assertion of *harmony* between the Bible and Teetotalism than to contend for his Teetotalism being *taught* in the Bible. But if he is satisfied with simply affirming this *harmony*, what means the placarded title of the lecture, " Teetotalism the plain teaching of the Bible" ? If only *harmony* is meant, why not say harmony ? for the English people are in the habit of judging of ideas by the words which express them : and if they are told that Dr. Lees only means harmony between the Bible and Teetotalism when he affirms this to be the plain teaching of that, they will probably conclude that Dr. Lees is only blinding them with worthless dust.

The question, with which the above quotation concludes, is a remarkable mode of convincing us, that Teetotalism is the plain teaching of the Bible. " Where do you find a single text," asks our Critic, " that, clearly and explicitly represents God as *contradicting* these doctrines ?" As though everything which is *not contradicted* in the Bible is the *plain teaching* of the Bible? Is Dr. Lees aware that the Bible, in no single text, clearly and explicitly denies that the Moon is made of silver farthings ? Will he therefore affirm that it is ?

On page 2 of the Reply, the author assumes that there is such perfect unity between the Bible and Teetotalism, that "*what one sounds, the other echoes in consonance and concord.*" Does our Critic expect those, who know what the Bible, and Teetotalism, really contain, to adopt such a hypothesis as this ? I for one, am very far from receiving it: and, I presume that there are but few who will not at once see the entire absurdity of it.

Further on in the same page, a quotation is given from my lecture, where I observe that "Teetotalism, with those who are in health, I believe to be nothing less in general than a wise method of economising health and money."

"Now if, as he asserts, the practice is really good—'*and nothing less, in general, than a wise method of economising health and money*'—it may be fairly asked of him, 'How is it that the Bible, which you say teaches the *whole* duty of man, has *not* taught this special piece of wisdom?'"

To this I reply, I have no idea that the Bible teaches every special piece of wisdom, *so called by Dr. Lees and his admirers;* and if they mean by Teetotalism entire "abstinence from toxic drink, and the discountenancing of *all* drinking customs, on the ground that alcohol is a *bad article*, not 'a good creature'; then, I say, neither Scripture nor Science will support them in that: for I believe, that is not special wisdom at all, but special nonsense. There are, however, many wise methods, and contrivances, for economising health and money, albeit they are not taught in the Bible. I may instance the East Lancashire Railway as one. But are all the plans and principles, upon which that Railway was constructed, plainly laid down in the Bible? I take it that the directors have too much understanding to be afraid of my sweeping their line, and all its locomotives into the sea, although I firmly maintain that the laying down of the East Lancashire Railway, and the construction of all the apparatus for the efficient working of it, is not the plain teaching of the Bible. I must not say, however (I might reasonably be called upon to explain if I did), that the plans adopted by those who formed the line were not in harmony with the Bible. But according to Dr. Lees' mode of reasoning, this, and every line of Railway is a blunder; for in writing in a local newspaper, January 8th last, he says, "God's plan is better than ours, and if ours be not the same, then Teetotalism is a blunder": as if every human invention is a blunder. Is it not the fact, that Dr. Lees himself is blundering?

Our Critic does me too much honour when he intimates that it is merely *my* affirmation that "the Bible teaches the whole duty of man." If he turns to Eccl. xii. 13, he may there read in our English version of the Scriptures as follows: "*Fear God, and keep His commandments: for this* is the whole duty of man." Here, then, we are informed what is our "whole duty" in very few words.

"The alleged discrepancy between the Bible and Teetotalism, Dr. Lees maintains to be subjective—i.e. in the minds of the presuming and pretentious interpreters alone, and is open to the old rebuke uttered by Galilei, against those who, in their self-conceit, placed their own crude and dogmatic interpretation on a level with the Divine word." (p. 2.)

What a felicitous condition of mind must our unpresuming and unpretending Doctor be in! Dear, humble man! He is a veritable Doctor of Philosophy; and never appears to dream that he should be regarded as one of those "presuming and pretentious interpreters" referred to. Let all England admire the meekness of Dr. Lees, who, in the foregoing extract, cherishes a feeling of thankfulness that he is not vain glorious, and rabid in his censures, like other men.

As for "the alleged discrepancy between the Bible and Teetotalism," I may observe, that it is useless for the writer of the Reply to attempt to fasten upon me the assertion of such a discrepancy, inasmuch as I distinctly stated, in my published Lecture, that I believe Teetotalism to be "*in entire harmony with the word of God.*" If by the term "discrepancy" we are to understand simply "disagreement, or contrariety;" and by Teetotalism, abstinence from strong drink as an ordinary beverage, and a discountenancing of its general use as a luxury; I can hardly conceive how any one can affirm a positive discrepancy between the Bible and such Teetotalism. The conduct of a pious and temperate Abstainer is evidently sanctioned, at least so long as he is in health. But if the Abstainer were to abstain in sickness, to the hindrance of his recovery, or the endangering of his life, or in cases where alcoholic stimulant might be really necessary to carry the system over a dangerous crisis, I believe that total abstinence, in such cases, would neither be expedient, nor right.

As Dr. Lees speaks of a *subjective discrepancy*, I would suggest, for his consideration, the possibility of a *subjective redundancy*, "—*i.e. in the minds of the presuming and pretentious interpreters* *alone, and open to the old rebuke uttered by Galilei against*" some who saw more in the cloud land of their own imagination than could be seen in the firmament of God's power: for it is recorded in the statements which are furnished of Galilei, and his times, that some of " his opponents found out five satellites for Jupiter instead of four; while one had the impudence to say that he actually saw nine satellites."* Query: Is not that which Dr. Lees professes to discover, as a full grown orb in the Heavens of Inspired Truth, a reflection of his own mind rather than that of the Divine Spirit? It seems to me, and I suspect it will appear to many others, that Dr. Lees has but a slender *objective* foundation for the assertion, " Teetotalism the plain teaching of the Bible." Let the public, however, who are acquainted with Dr. Lees' sayings, judge as to the proper application of Galilei's rebuke, which is to be flung " against those who, in their self-conceit, place their own crude and dogmatic interpretation on a level with the Divine word......... making for themselves a shield of simulated zeal for religion, and degrading the Holy Scriptures into the *instrument of private opinions.*" Our critic himself has made these last words, which, appear to be a quotation from Galilei, emphatic. It is to be hoped, therefore, that a suitable impression of their importance is deepened on his *own* mind. For his further advantage, I will quote another declaration, said to have been made by the same Italian philosopher, and also hurled, I suppose, against certain " presuming and pretentious interpreters," when he stated "*that the object of the Scriptures was to teach men the way of salvation, and not to instruct them in Astronomy, for the acquiring of which they were endowed with sufficient natural faculties.*" This was a saying worthy of Galilei. Putting the word " Teetotalism" for " Astronomy," I commend it to the serious consideration of Dr. Lees.

The quotations which follow are characteristic of our peppery Reply. The fault which is condemned in them is, that I have not done homage to Dr. Lees' " tracts, pamphlets, and volumes." Not having consulted these, nor cared to know what is contained in them, I am charged with publishing in my lecture a " *monstrous substitution and perversion of terms;*" and my looking to the

* Article ' Galilei,' Penny Cyclopædia.

Bible for something like a Divine prohibition of strong drink is exhibited as an "*impudent evasion* of the real propositions of Dr. Lees." Now it might have seemed reasonable enough to most people, to expect that, if Teetotalism be "the plain teaching of the Bible," it would be enforced by a plain command. Not knowing, at the time when I delivered my lecture, that it was possible to acquaint myself with Dr. Lees' argument for "the plain teaching," I was "*impudent*" enough to consult my own judgment about the matter. But our very bilious Critic seems to wax wrath at this.

"Mr. Williams," he says, " equally blunders over the proposition to be debated with the Teetotallers."

Who had said anything about my wanting to debate with the Teetotallers? I made no promise to debate with them. But although I have not shrunk from debate when it was thrust upon me, my object, in the delivery of my lecture, was not to contend against Teetotalism, nor with Teetotallers, but to show the error of a false proposition, which, I presume, most Teetotallers, as they know their Bibles, will reject as promptly as I have rejected it.

"He represents it (i. e. the proposition) as being,—whether there is in *the Bible* a *universal precept, commanding* all men to abstain, at all times and in all places, from intoxicating drinks?"

I certainly did not say so: although before endorsing the statement, "Teetotalism the plain teaching of the Bible," something like a universal precept, or plain enforcement, might be properly looked for. If Dr. Lees does not mean to affirm that Teetotalism is a duty binding upon all men, it will be well for him distinctly to say so. In that case further argument will be needless. But if Teetotalism be a moral duty, and it be plainly taught in the Bible as a moral duty, what, I ask, should we expect but a plain command, or a statement to the effect that it *is* a moral duty? But it is worth something to know, that our Critic, who evidently desires to find Teetotalism taught in the Bible, has himself so little faith in the fact of its being taught there, that he tumbles into a positive *furor* at the very idea of looking into the Bible for a plain command.

"Never," he says, "was there put forth a more monstrous substitution and perversion of terms; never a more impudent evasion of the real propositions of Dr. Lees."

But the beauty perceptible in this indignant climacteric, is enhanced by the fact that, in order to get at it, he puts words into my mouth, or into my lecture, which I never repeated, and which I never wrote. I have not anywhere said that, "*the proposition to be debated*," was "*whether there is in the Bible a universal precept, commanding all men to abstain*," etc.

It has not been my design to controvert what Dr. Lees has written. But it may be well to take, as a sample of his reasoning, the "seven progressive propositions," to which we are treated in the reply.

"1. The Bible *represents* intoxicating drink as a bad thing."

I do not believe such a statement. That the Bible represents the *abuse* of intoxicating drink as evil and only evil, no one can deny. But Dr. Lees, I think, has altogether failed to establish in his printed lecture, that the drink itself is a *bad thing*, or that the Bible represents it as such.

"2. Represents Teetotalism as the observance of the Law of Food."

The attempt to show that the Bible does this, is again an egregious failure, and, with the great bulk of thinking men, I am persuaded, will be regarded as injurious to the cause of Teetotalism: for the attempt to prop up a good cause with arguments which are utterly fallacious, is in general to undermine it.

"3. As practised by individuals and societies under Divine sanction."

This is not to be denied. But, that Teetotalism was "practised by individuals and societies under Divine sanction," is by no means sufficient to establish, that the practice was therefore obligatory upon others, besides the classes referred to. And certainly this proposition, by itself, is not enough to establish that "Teetotalism is the plain teaching of the Bible."

"4. As a physiological law, or truth."

If Teetotalism is to be regarded "as a physiological law, or truth," it must be on the ground of our common observation, combined with the deductions of physiological science. But the Bible says not a word about the laws of physiology. How then does it represent Teetotalism as a physiological law, or truth? Dr. Lees will doubtless be ready to tell us that Sampson was a very strong man, and he was a Teetotaller. But we cannot deduce a law from a single example. Well, but Dr. Lees shows that the Nazarites, according to the Scripture, were ruddy and beautiful. Daniel, and his Jewish brethren, who preferred plain pulse and water, were fairer and in better condition than those who took the portion of the king's meat, and the wine which he drank. I gladly accept these Scripture facts, as a plain testimony in favour of a frugal and abstinent diet. There is, unquestionably, in all this, a close and delightful concord between Scripture and the teachings of physiology. And Dr. Lees may doubtless contribute to the advancement of religion, and science, and morality, by asserting this *harmony*. But to say, that Scripture itself " *represents Teetotalism as a physiological law or truth,*" is to go beyond the mark.

"5. As a Divine remedy for Intemperance."

Dr. Lees refers, in proof of this, to the prohibition administered to the priests when about to officiate in the tabernacle, to the effect that they were not to drink wine nor strong drink—Lev. x. I think that we are justified in drawing the inference that this was a Divine appointment for preventing the stupifying effects frequently produced by intoxicating drinks. But this remedy was not what we should now call Teetotalism. The plan here appointed was that of *temporary* abstinence, which is not Teetotalism. How then can it be concluded from this, that the Bible represents *Teetotalism* as a Divine remedy for Intemperance? When pressed with this objection, the Doctor tries to escape the difficulty by saying: "We do *not* apply it *as* a positive prohibition to all men,—but regard it as a special law involving a universally applicable principle." But surely, this is something very different from the original proposition, which says, " The Bible *represents Teetotalism* as a Divine remedy for Intemperance." These are large words signifying more than the Bible declares. In fact, Dr. Lees gives us here as elsewhere, in his published lecture, principles and inferences built up on all sorts of authorities: and I believe that many of his principles are accordant with the teachings of the Word of God.* But when he goes beyond this to show that therefore these are the plain teaching of the Bible, he expresses himself in such a way as to render himself unintelligible to those who are not ripe for his sophistications. For when Dr. Lees, or any one else, blinds us with empty abuse, instead of solid argument, to make us believe that the words, "in harmony with," mean the same as, "the plain teaching of," it does appear to me as objectionable a mode of sophisticating as any one can be capable of.

"6. As a preparation for spiritual life."

Here is another proposition to express Dr. Lees' own *conception* of the probable design with which God gave the law pertaining to Priests and Nazarites. But the Bible nowhere expresses that design. If Dr. Lees had said that the Bible represents Teetotalism as a preparation for long life, for beauty of appearance, for bodily strength, for a clear understanding, for a discriminating judgment, or for the enjoyment of the world, it might have been as correct as to say that Teetotalism is represented in the Scriptures as a preparation for spiritual life. The Doctor thinks it quite enough to refer to the doctrines of ancient Pagans, Christian Fathers, Italians, etc., in proof of "wine and good cheer exciting to impurity," and he can then conclude, that the design of the law enjoining abstinence on Priests and Nazarites, was to prepare for spiritual life: *ergo*, "*the Bible represents Teetotalism as a preparation for spiritual life.*"

"7. As originally inspired by God himself."

What was inspired? The law for the Priests and Nazarites. But with that law there was united the inspired permission, that those who were not about to officiate as Priests in the Sanctuary, and who were not under the vow of a Nazarite, might take what Priests and Nazarites were forbidden, during specified times, to use. But in view of special evils with which our own age is afflicted, we should ask for special measures of reform; and here is our legitimate argument for a Temperance-loving Teetotalism.

---

* Not this, however, that Teetotalism is a Divine remedy for intemperance. God's remedy for all Intemperance, and for sin in its every form, must be found in those holy principles, and powerful motives, which are expressed in the gospel of His Son.

Our Critic wishes to have it believed that I have manufactured some proposition for Dr. Lees. What this manufactured proposition is, he does not say. But here are his words.

> "What makes this manufacture of a proposition for Dr. Lees still more reprehensible, is the fact, that one of the mottoes on his title page distinctly repudiates the doctrine which Mr. Williams represents as being held by the Teetotal advocate."

I had neither seen the title page nor the mottoes, before giving my lecture. The book which I examined was the Bible. And our Critic seems mightily offended at it. He thinks, I suppose, that I should have known what Dr. Lees had said, and that, without questioning Dr. Lees, I ought not to have said anything on the subject of Teetotalism and the Bible. I am even lectured upon "the impertinence of such a proceeding." I cannot wonder that when our Critic came to this, he should have been reminded of the cuttle fish. It would have been as well if he had remembered also what he had told his readers, on the first page, about my friend and I going into print without consulting the authority of Dr. Lees: which was the truth. But after stating that, it is a very plain piece of impertinence to talk about my manufacturing a proposition for Dr. Lees. I manufactured nothing on Dr. Lees' account. I did not even mention Dr. Lees' name in the whole of my lecture: and Dr. Lees knew very well, because he was plainly informed, that there was not, in the whole of my lecture, a single allusion to him, or to any thing which he had said. Does the replier mean to say that I manufactured the proposition, "Teetotalism the plain teaching of the Bible?" and that that was the "*man of straw*," which I had stuffed up? Verily, that was the work of Dr. Lees, or else of his friendly admirers. But I entirely deny that I represented any doctrine "as being held by the teetotal advocate," beside the one which appeared in the advertisement of Dr. Lees' lecture. And I had too much respect for Teetotal advocates in general to saddle them with that.

But the reference in the Reply seems to be to a proposition so-called, which is plainly *manufactured for me*. This proposition comes in the form of a question, which is not mine, but the composition, I suppose, of our clever Critic; viz., "Whether there is in *the Bible a universal precept*, COMMANDING all men to abstain, at all times, and in all places, from intoxicating drinks?" Our Replier, albeit he is employed to discuss matters in print, is evidently fast for want of something to find fault with. Accordingly, he will have it that I have represented this, which I have not so represented at all, as " *the proposition to be debated* with the Teetotallers." The words "represent," "represented," "representation," are very convenient with the author of the Reply: for he thinks he can make it appear that either the Bible or any other writing represents things according to the colour of the spectacles which he is pleased to look through, when it might be undesirable to use plainer English in saying that such a thing is expressed. Now any one may look from one end of my lecture to the other, and it will be seen that I have no where stated the foregoing as the question, or as the proposition to be debated. The words in which that question is couched are not mine. But it is thought, perhaps, that I meant something like what is here expressed for me, and that therefore this *manufactured proposition* may answer well enough to *represent* what I intended. I did not suppose, however, and certainly I never intimated that such was *the proposition* to be debated. It will be seen in my lecture that I have not confined myself to the question of command or prohibition. I have dealt with the lessons furnished by example, by the true signification of words, by proverbs, and by scripture symbols. In fact, to use the large words of our critic, with whom words seem to be frequently something more than counters, I have dealt, as I was able in the time allotted, with "the history and the criticism, the providence and the philology of the Bible:" and I can truly say that I have not found them "at variance" with each other.

But in reference to this manufactured proposition which our Critic has propounded, he says:

" A 'man of straw' is stuffed up by the 'Shepherd', and the 'Sheep' are requested to admire the skill of the fabricator in setting fire to it before their innocent faces!"

All of which I take to be a very sheepish joke on the part of the shepherd who has really stuffed up this 'man of straw;' especially as his conscience is so transparent as to admit of our seeing its inner operations by the words, "*this manufacture of a proposition.*" It is to be hoped that our Critic will cease this manufacture of propositions, and this mode of stuffing up combustible materials, lest he himself should be again burnt; for I take it that they who read are not sheep, but intelligent, thinking men.

"Surely," he says, "no man of the commonest education can honestly make the words 'lesson, teaching, or representation', the equivalents of universal precept and command.'"

I suppose not: but who does? Is it, however, the very same author who thus contends for a distinction between the words 'teaching' and 'precept,' that scoffs, on the first page of the reply, at the distinction between the Bible teaching, and the Bible harmonizing with, Teetotalism? What extraordinary methods of discrimination our philosopher must have, if he supposes that the idea of teaching is not as much allied with the word 'precept' or 'command,' as with the expression 'harmonizing with!'

He asks:

"Can or does God teach *merely* by verbal commands, or positive prohibitions?"

It is true, that God does teach *sometimes* by such methods; and is it not allowable to ask whether the Bible teaches Teetotalism by these, or any other methods? Does not Dr. Lees himself lay as much stress as he possibly can, upon the commands, and prohibitions, addressed to Priests and Nazarites?

Our author speaks in the next paragraph about "the ruse of the cuttle fish," and its "sepian inkiness." "Hic nigrae fucus loliginis." "Here is the dye of the black cuttle-fish." This may be more intelligible to some if we quote the following from the Imperial Dictionary. "CUTTLE, CUTTLE FISH. (Sax. *cudele,* from the sense of withdrawing or *hiding.*) A genus of Mollusca, called Sepia. They have small arms, with serrated cups, by which they lay fast hold of anything. They have also two tentacula longer than the arms; the mouth is in the centre of the arms, and is horny, and hooked like the bill of a hawk. They have a little bladder under the throat, from which, when pursued, they throw out a black liquor that darkens the water, by which means they escape. Hence *cuttle* is used for a foul-mouthed fellow; one who blackens another's character."

After his telling reference to "the ruse of the cuttle fish," and "seeking to hide the plain facts in the sepian inkiness of his criticisms," the writer of the Reply assumes a tone of injured authority, and "*cannot withhold*" his "*stern rebuke.*" May I ask the writer who waxes so very pompous in the eyes of Christendom if it would not increase the drollery of all this, supposing, the next time he balances himself to hurl his rebukes, he would have the simple honesty to tell us his name. In the meantime, I would not for a moment deprive our Critic of the gratification which he experiences in rebuking me: and if it be any relief or pleasure to him, he may vie in vehemence with the whistling tempest.

"Mr. Williams," says our critic, "mistakes the method of proof."

That is to say, Mr. W. has not adopted Dr. Lees' method of proving Teetotalism to be the plain teaching of the Bible.

"The lecture to which his own ought to have been a rejoinder—(for he has replied only to his own perversion of its placarded title)—establishes the seven propositions upon the plain words of the authorized version, and carefully avoids *critical* disquisition founded on the original Hebrew."

Our Critic seems to be annoyed that my lecture was not a rejoinder to Dr. Lees'. It makes no difference to him, perhaps, that I did not know at the time what the Doctor's lecture was. But I may be allowed to affirm that, in general, Ministers of the Gospel have other duties to attend to, beside giving rejoinders to everything which may be reported to them as declared by itinerating lecturers. My duty was simply and faithfully to declare what is said in the Scriptures; and, although I did feel it right to refer to one or two statements, which were made by a Mr. Sandeman, in the discussion which followed a preceding discourse on Temperance, my published lecture was not intended in any sense to be a rejoinder. My friend, Mr. Wilkinson, and I, agreed to enquire for ourselves, " Is Teetotalism the plain teaching of the Bible?" and to make known the result of our investigation. And will Dr. Lees, or any one else, presume to tell us, that we must not do that without consulting him?

What is meant by the expression, "*his own perversion of its placarded title*," I will leave to the decision of the public. The placarded title of Dr. Lees' lecture was this: "Teetotalism the plain teaching of the Bible." That this was a perversion, or distortion, from the original title of Dr. Lees' lecture, "On the harmony of Teetotalism with the Divine Word," few perhaps will deny. But I had nothing to do with this perversion. Neither the Curate nor myself issued the placards announcing Dr. Lees' lectures. But when we saw the proposition, which we instantly conceived to be an objectionable one, we said that it really deserved our attention. Although it would not be possible for us to hear the lecture of Dr. Lees, we felt that it would be dutiful, not to shirk the question, but honestly to ask, "Is Teetotalism the plain teaching of the Bible?" For convenience' sake, I agreed to take up the enquiry, Is it the teaching of the Old Testament? Mr. Wilkinson promised to follow with the question, Is it the teaching of the New? But, I suppose, the charge of perversion is to be fastened upon me, because I have not examined the whole of the Bible in a single lecture. A query naturally suggests itself here. Are the facts and logic of the Reply worthy of the patronage of the Great Harwood Temperance Society?

As for Dr. Lees seeking to establish his "seven propositions upon the plain words of the authorised version, and carefully avoiding *critical* disquisition founded on the original Hebrew," there may not be very much credit due to him for that. It appears that, when it suits his purpose, he is as ready to appeal to the original text of Scripture as any one, and when it does not suit him, perhaps, he "*carefully avoids it.*"

"Now, if Dr. Lees made good *his* position from the plain *facts* of Scripture history, how can the proof be got rid of by disputing the Bible *terms* for wine? Unless Mr. Williams believes that the history and the criticism, the providence and the philology, of the Bible, are at variance, he cannot fail to perceive the impertinence of such a proceeding. Was he simply throwing dust in the eyes of his people, and thus in imitating the ruse of the cuttle fish, seeking to hide *the plain facts* in the sepian inkiness of his criticisms? To engender doubt, instead of conciliating difficulties and removing discrepancies—where, as in *two fields of truth*, none can *really* exist—is not, at any rate, in harmony with the functions of a true christian pastor; but we cannot withhold our stern rebuke when this perverse ingenuity is exhibited on behalf of appetites and customs which are blighting the fairest blossoms of Christianity, and spreading disaster and desolation throughout the land."

To begin here at the beginning:

"Now, IF Dr. Lees made good his position from the plain facts of Scripture history."

Yes, IF! It was well that our Critic had the modesty to insert that IF. But in the following sentence he forgets, apparently, that he had inserted it; and proceeds as if there could not be a particle of doubt, that so clever a man as Dr. Lees could make the Bible say almost anything. On looking, however, into the Doctor's printed lecture since the publication of my own, I find that he has not been content with appealing to the simple testimony of the Bible. The boast is altogether a vain one, that Dr. Lees "establishes his seven propositions upon the plain words of the authorized version." I am fully convinced that he has not established them in any way. As to "making good *his* position from the plain facts of Scripture history," it is evident, that Dr. Lees does not even pretend, in his lecture, to limit himself to the plain facts of the Bible. In that lecture we have a string of the following authorities. They are here marked according to the pages where they are named: Sallust, p. 4. Jones of Nayland, p. 5. Bishop Lowth, Porphyry, the *Clavis Symbolica*, Philo, Clement, Professor Kidd, p. 6. Benson, the Vedas of the Brahmans, the Zendavesta of the Persians, Empedocles, Socrates, Siddharta, Pythagoras, Zoroaster, and Epicurus, p. 7. There is even a greater number of names on the eighth page. Altogether, we have, in the thirty-four pages of Dr. Lees' published lecture, about two or three score of authorities, Pagan, and Christian; among whom are Poets, Historians, Philosophers, and Divines; all ranged in delightful harmony with Dr. Lees, to show that Teetotalism must be "in harmony with," or (what suits our Critic's taste the better) that it is "the plain teaching of the Bible." Of course, in order to harmony, there must be no discord: and our printing Doctor wills it, that discords for the time shall cease to be heard; and these are put out of court until judgment is given in reply to imaginary opponents.

An instructive mode of reasoning is contained on p. 7 of his lecture just referred to, where having asserted that "the Bible represents intoxicating drink" as an "evil," he says: "It would be strange indeed if it did *not*,—even were we to regard it merely as a book preserving to us the highest moral lessons of antiquity, or *to place it upon a par with the Vedas of the Brahmans, the Zenda-*

vesta of the Persians, or the Golden verses of Empedocles." Assuming that the Bible embraces the collective wisdom of these ancient compositions, as well as that of all the other authorities which are quoted, our author proceeds from Homer and Zoroaster, downwards, to an engraving in the Paris 'Illustrated News,' and drags from all, the conclusion, that the Bible teaches Teetotalism. Nothing could seem more natural, or appropriate, in view of these manifold quotations which are made in Dr. Lees' lecture, and by which he makes "*good his position from the plain facts of Scripture history,*" than the question of our Critic: "Was he simply throwing dust in the eyes of the people, and thus in imitating the ruse of the cuttle fish, seeking to hide *the plain facts* in the sepian inkiness of his criticisms?"

With regard to the belief, as alluded to, "that the history and the criticisms, the providence and the philology, of the Bible, are at variance," I will explain, that I believe them all to be at variance only with all truth, imposture, and intemperance, whether of speech or anything else. But for our Critic to saddle upon me the consequence of a *petitio principii*, which is of his own choosing, is a mode of replying to my lecture, which needs but little refutation.

And now, about *engendering doubt*, "*instead of conciliating difficulties and removing discrepancies—where, as in two fields of truth, none can really exist.*" What does our Critic mean? How can any one conciliate what does not exist to be conciliated, or remove what does not exist to be removed? But here, in our author's reply, is an asterisk pointing to a foot note. And there we find a discrepancy to be removed which does not elsewhere exist. Our ingenious Critic, in professing to give a quotation from my lecture, makes me to say at p. 27: "I am exceedingly dull in apprehending the truth." Is that the way in which Dr. Lees quotes Scripture to make it teach Teetotalism? But I may remind our Replier, that there is a difference between truth, and the truthfulness of his inferences and quotations. Many beside myself may be slow to apprehend the latter.

The two fields of truth in the view of our far-seeing Critic seem to be the Bible and Dr. Lees: and he tells us that, "to engender doubt instead of conciliating difficulties and removing discrepancies

—where, as in *two fields of truth*, none can *really* exist—is not, at any rate, in harmony with the functions of a true Christian pastor." Is it then a sin against the pastoral office even to question the infallibility of Dr. Lees? Is it impossible that there should be any discrepancy between him and the Bible? In that case, the author of the reply may think it a pity that the Doctor's peculiar meekness and modesty should restrain him from going a step further. Why not give his works to the world as a substitute for the Bible, and declare at once that everything in Divine law, and human morals, is invalid which is not sanctioned by the authority of Dr. Lees? He may then, with greater consistency, refuse to withhold his "stern rebuke when this perverse ingenuity" of appealing to the Sacred Scriptures is resorted to. If the United Kingdom could only be formed into a kind of Utah territory, with Dr. Lees, instead of Brigham Young, at the head of it; then might Clergymen, Independent Ministers, and Temperance advocates, be speedily drilled into subjection to the presiding spirit of the "*Truth Seeker*" office: then might the terrors of the Westminster Court of Exchequer cease, and slander plumed with a diploma from Giessen, dance frantically to the tune of "*stern rebuke*."

Our Critic wishes it to be distinctly understood that my non-admission of Dr. Lees' statement, "Teetotalism the plain teaching of the Bible," is the fruit of a "*perverse ingenuity*," "exhibited on behalf of appetites and customs which are blighting the fairest blossoms of Christianity, and spreading disaster and desolation throughout the land." But I cannot accept this award as to my ingenuity. Our anonymous author is too generous. The perverse ingenuity complained of is simple honesty. I have been sincerely desirous to know what is the Scripture teaching on Teetotalism; and if Dr. Lees, or any one else, will tell me more than I have yet been able to learn of this matter, I shall be thankful to receive instruction. But I cannot consent to tell falsehood, though it should be to please Dr. Lees; nor can I consent to endorse arguments which appear to be full of logical blundering. Must we, in advocating Dr. Lees' form of Teetotalism, speak the very opposite of our convictions? If so, then his Teetotalism may perish for me: but I will go on speaking what I know and believe to be the truth:

for sure I am, that truth can never be opposed to morality. But of all ingenuities for bringing both the Bible and Teetotalism into contempt, I believe *that* ingenuity to be the most perverse, and uningenuous, which will pretend to drag from the Book of God statements nowhere supported in it, and which will then hurl rebuke and vilification against any one, who fails to admire the process by which this is said to be done.

Undoubtedly, it is the duty of Dr. Lees, as of every Christian pastor, to promote the interests of Truth, and Religion, and Morality; and at the same time to repress, by all legitimate means, those "appetites and customs which are blighting the very fairest blossoms of Christianity, and spreading disaster and desolation throughout the land." I shall not therefore be driven by Dr. Lees, nor by any one else, to oppose Teetotalism, the practice of which, in multitudes of instances, is most beneficial. But it is important to be borne in mind, that there are other rules, beside the law of Teetotalism, for preventing moral disaster and desolation. And in self defence, I may be allowed to affirm that I have never so far vilified an honest and upright teetotal advocate, as to say, that he "has been often seen narcotically and helplessly intoxicated," nor threatened to "lecture on the evidence from Caithness to Cornwall," nor talked of justice being done in the way of inflicting punishment, "even if the Temperance heavens fall." If I had done all this, beside attempting to damage the character and influence of several preachers of religion, and morality, there might have been some show of reason for the lofty indignation which rebukes "this perverse ingenuity."

But then Dr. Lees is a thorough advocate of Teetotalism! Yes; and well known among Teetotallers. Let the following extract from the *Metropolitan Temperance Intelligencer*, dated September, 1845, bear testimony to this.

"And, secondly, we can assure *The Truth Seeker and Temperance Advocate,* that *he* is not very highly respected by that same body; that he is not regarded as 'infallible;' and that his present course is by no means calculated to elicit the TRUTH, or to advocate, with success, genuine TEMPERANCE. It is, rather, the opinion of those whose opinions are worth knowing, that THE TRUTH is likely to be stifled, and the progress of TEMPERANCE greatly retarded, and RELIGION grossly caricatured, by his present 'Seeker,' and his projected 'Magazine for the People'. His posture, so far from being that of a docile, ingenuous, honest 'Seeker of Truth,' is rather that of the self-complacent, pedantic, arrogant polemic, who

> 'Spikes up his inch of reason on the point
> Of philosophic wit, called argument;
> And then, exulting in his taper, cries,
> Behold the sun! and, Indian-like, adore!'"

At the beginning of the next paragraph in the reply, our Critic returns to the attack upon his favourite 'man of straw.' Having formed it according to his mind, and expended nearly a page of controversy upon it, he comes to it again, with as much surprise as if he had not observed it before.

"But the most signal of all the instances of theological blundering that Mr. Williams has fallen into, is the misapprehension under which he labours as to the possibility of the Old Testament furnishing the proposition so abundantly challenged, viz: 'A command for total abstinence always and for everybody, all the world over!!!"

This creature of our Critic's imagination, which is improperly represented as a quotation from my lecture, has seemed to grow upon him since he dealt with it before; and, as if to denote his astonishment, there are now three notes of exclamation inserted after it; or, it may be, that they are introduced according to the printer's conscience: for, in order to this most signal instance of "*theological blundering*" being made more signal, I am exhibited again as saying what I did not say, and what is nowhere to be found in my lecture. But the well-balanced mind of the Replier might have thought that, as he had taken the liberty to leave out the beginning of a sentence, that I might seem to stultify myself in the foot note, he would make up the weight of the next quotation by prefixing the words, "*A command for :*"—all this, on the principle that exchange is no robbery. Moreover it is *truth-seeking* honesty. I had asked the question at the beginning of my lecture: "What do they (the Teetotallers) mean?"—i.e. by Teetotalism? "Total abstinence always, and for everybody, all the world over?" It seems from the Reply, that the proposal of this question, connected as it is with an enquiry as to what the Jewish law taught in the matter of abstinence, is "the most signal of all the instances of theological blundering that Mr. Williams has fallen into." This I take to be a compliment: for, if the instance now given of my theological blundering be the most signal, it is certainly a weak case for our Critic to ground an attack upon. I merely asked a question as to what Dr. Lees' friends meant by Teetotalism. But I was really not so ignorant of the Scriptures as to fall into the "*misapprehension*" which is spoken of: for I did not believe it possible that either the Old Testament, or the New, could be understood as furnishing a command for total abstinence, binding upon every one.

"And we are even seriously asked the amazing question, 'How is it, then, that the law of Moses should specify only some *particular* times, and some particular individuals among the *Jewish* nation?' How is it, we retort, that a professional expounder of Scripture, has remained to this day ignorant of the foremost fact in Scriptural exegesis—namely, that Mosaism *was* Mosaism, and not Universalism? He has really asked us to tell him how it is that Jewism is not Gentilism —that is, Christianity!'"

Most sapient Sir! As you have put to me a question, I, your obedient servant, would reply as follows.—So ignorant have I been —so dull of apprehension, if you will—that to this day I knew not that Gentilism is Christianity. But a fool sometimes may puzzle a Doctor of Philosophy: and therefore I am disposed to press the question, which you, Sir, have not answered: that question, not being, how is it that Jewism is not Gentilism, nor how is it that Dr. Lees is not a Jew, but simply this: How is it, if Teetotalism be, according to the teaching of Scripture as you imply, morally binding upon all, that even the *Jewish* law, which was stricter in many of its requirements than the Christian—that even that Jewish law—only specified the duty of abstaining from wines and strong drinks for some particular times, and some particular individuals?—for the priest when he went to minister in the sanctuary, and for the Nazarite during the time of his vow?" And I press this question the more; inasmuch as Dr. Lees, when it suits his purpose, takes *the sanction of the law of Moses* with regard to the Priests and Nazarites. In the *Accrington Free Press* of Feb. 5, 1859, a letter, signed *F. R. Lees*, contains the following in reply to the Rev. Mr. Wilkinson:

TEETOTALISM FOUNDED ON REASON.

> "And for my part, when I look at the signal instances of Scripture Teetotalism commanded by God to His Priesthood, His Nazarites, and His strong champions and favourites, it would seem a waste of time to *argue* with a person who denies that Teetotalism is *God's plan*."

Total abstinence, we admit, *was* God's plan for some particular individuals, and some special circumstances. But will Dr. Lees be content with a system of Teetotalism which shall affect only Priests and Nazarites? Teetotallers want a broader measure, adapted to the wants of our English community, and to check the enormous vices of the nineteenth century. And if it be affirmed that Teetotalism is the plan of reason and common sense, there can be no disparagement in this. Is not reason the gift of God, as well as the Bible? Are we not to be guided by reason, as well as by Scripture in the varying circumstances of life? Must we wait for a Divine law, before we inveigh against the general and pernicious use of tobacco, or proceed to the suppression of the Opium traffic? Must we ask, before demanding a plan of legislative reform for the country, whether the Bible teaches it? If not; and it be admitted that God has made nothing, and appointed no natural law, but with a wise intent; then, what can Dr. Lees be thinking about when he sends the following to a local Newspaper?*

> "I moreover asserted, and reassert, that whoever predicates that the *use* of alcoholic beverages has the authority of God, and that Teetotalism is the 'invention of man,' to all intents and purposes *opposes* Teetotalism. God's plan is better than ours, and if ours be not the same, then Teetotalism is a blunder."

Is there any logic or philosophy in this? To me it seems almost inconceivable that a man in Dr. Lees' position should be capable of stultifying himself with such a mode of writing. Doubtless, God's plan *is better than ours* where He is pleased to give us His plan. But what are we to do when we are left to work out our own plan? Go back, the Doctor tells us, to an obsolete plan. The ark, which saved Noah and his family at the time of the deluge, was God's plan. Suppose that Dr. Lees is conversing with a ship builder, we may fancy him using these very large words, "God's plan is better than ours, and if ours be not the same, our *ship building* is a blunder." Query, Doctor: Is it not God's plan that we should

---

* Accrington Free Press, Jan. 8, 1859. Letter signed F. R. Lees.

build every legitimate reform on a broad and sufficient foundation of fact? And is it not very like attempting to build a castle in the air, if you take the top-stone of Tectotalism, which perhaps is its most beauteous ornament; the fact that it harmonizes with inspired truth; and confound this with an expression which conveys to ordinary minds the notion of a new *basis* for Teetotalism? In his "Lecture on the harmony of Teetotalism with the Divine word," Dr. Lees very properly states, that "Teetotallers do not seek to base their doctrines upon the Bible; but are satisfied to affirm their harmony with it." But as he grows older, Dr. Lees is not satisfied with the assertion of this harmony. He may vituperate as much as he pleases about the puerile distinction between the Bible teaching Teetotalism, and the Bible harmonizing with it: but the Doctor is not so quicksighted as I have taken him to be, if he does not perceive the inevitable impression which is made on the popular mind by the statement, " *Teetotalism the plain teaching of the Bible.*" They who reverence the Word of God take the *rule of its* TEACHING *as the broad basis* of their holiest principles: but they do not always rest their conduct on what is merely in harmony with the Bible, nor do they think it necessary to do so. Dr. Lees knows all this as well as any man in Britain. And to publish the statement now quoted; " Teetotalism the plain teaching of the Bible ;" and to follow it with the declaration that Teetotalism is a blunder, if it be not God's plan, is very much the same as if the Doctor should kick with all his might against an Egyptian pyramid, crying out : " 'Tis a blunder that this pyramid is reposing so securely, with its ample base on the broad surface of the earth: I shall kick it over so that it may stand upon its apex. The top-stone is in beautiful harmony with the heaven beyond. Therefore I, Dr. Lees, will have it, that it is too ethereal and Divine a thing to rest like other vulgar contrivances on an earthly foundation." We cannot doubt that the Divine appointment with regard to the temporary abstinence of Priests and Nazarites was founded in Infinite wisdom. But the tectotal system, which we, as Englishmen, would seek to carry out, and which happily prevails in this nineteenth century, has no more to do with the law for Priests and Nazarites than the ordinary diet of a Chinese mandarin has to do with the prescriptions of an English physician. There may be ingredients which are common to both: but *the plan* is essentially different.

In reference to the declaration of the New Testament, "*There is nothing unclean of itself*," which I quoted at the beginning of my lecture, from Paul's epistle to the Romans, the Reply says as follows:

"This was spoken of ceremonial uncleanness, and to apply it for ignoring the *physical* qualities of agents like opium, alcohol, and tobacco, is to pervert it."

I do not believe that this assertion of Paul is to be understood, necessarily, and exclusively, of ceremonial uncleanness. The epistle, from which these words are quoted, was addressed, not only to Jewish, but also to Gentile Christians at Rome. In the early part of the 14th chapter, the Apostle refers to the scruples of certain vegetarians. "One," he said, "believeth that he may eat all things: another, who is weak, eateth herbs." The inspired writer goes on from this to observe: " Let every man be fully persuaded in his own mind:" and at the 14th verse of the same chapter, in continuation of his argument, he tells the Roman converts, that "there is nothing common, or unclean, of itself." The Apostle might have had in view the scruples, which owed their origin to the ceremonial law of the Jews, as well as those which were awakened by heathen superstitions, or a false philosophy. But I presume that the Apostle *meant what he wrote*. True, the writer of the Reply does not seem to relish the passage, because it does not square with his peculiar views. He would have us believe that the statement must be received with extreme caution, or that it has no lesson for us Gentiles; and he proceeds to intimate what is plainly a contradiction of all Revelation, and true science; that some things *are* in themselves to be now regarded as common, or unclean; and that we must exclude from the category of clean substances, opium, alcohol, and tobacco. If our Critic be true, and Paul be a liar, is it not passing strange that some qualifying clause should not have been inserted somewhere in the New Testament, to the effect that Paul had made a mistake, and that opium, etc., etc., were not to be regarded as the products of a good, but an evil spirit? For myself, I beg leave to state that the substances named by the Replier, are no more unclean in themselves than is the pen with which he writes down his wretched philosophy. The evil results of the chewing, drinking, smoking, and writing, may be all alike apparent. But any man making the slightest pretence to the knowledge of Science should know that "*the physical qualities of agents like opium, alcohol, and tobacco*," can never be productive of injury, apart from that perversion of taste and judgment, which appropriates the gifts of God to improper uses.

"Moreover, it equally contradicts St. Paul, who speaks of 'wine wherein is excess,' and Solomon, who declares that 'wine' is 'a mocker'; and it does so, whether we understand 'much' or 'little' wine to be meant, since SOMETHING excites the condition wherein 'the eyes look upon strange women, and the heart utters perverse things': and are not such states *morally* unclean? When men, or ministers, so plead—

"'Tis *License* they mean, when they cry Liberty.'

May it please you, Sir, I am not pleading here for License or Liberty: but am wishful to see the truth, whether you give the license or not. And one must see very clearly, I think, by your quotations from Solomon that " wine is a mocker" *when men become intoxicated with it*, and that Solomon spake of the vice and ignominy connected with drunkenness, when he said: " At the last it biteth like a serpent, and stingeth like an adder. Thine eyes shall behold strange women," etc. It is the sin of *excess*, whether it be in the way of gluttony, or drunkenness, which is morally unclean. And it is really pitiable to find our Critic, who pretends to know something, endeavouring to fasten upon a *liquid* the charge of *excess*. No doubt excess *comes* by the *drinking* of wine; though I am by no means prepared to admit that this is in every instance. It was not excess, for a sober and abstinent Teetotaller to take *a little* for his often infirmities. And he who so far alters the standard of moral virtue, and confounds right and wrong, as to include those who take the smallest quantity of wine, whether in health or under infirmity, in one sweeping condemnation with the drunkard, is one who gives the greatest license to debauchery.

The word rendered *excess* in Eph. 5: 18, where Paul says, "Be not drunk with wine wherein (or whereby) is excess," plainly signifies what is *morally wrong;* as *lust, dissoluteness of living.* Properly speaking, the Greek word *asotia* (excess) denotes the life of a sot—the life or habits of one who is *asotos*: i.e. one given up to luxury, and profligacy. Will any man in his senses predicate all this of a substance which is without life? But there can be no reasonable doubt, I think, that in the passage under consideration, we should read *whereby*, or *by which*, instead of *wherein*. We should then have the passage as follows: "Be not drunk with wine, *whereby* is excess." Mac Knight, who is regarded as a most judicious commentator, gives the passage thus: "And be not drunk with wine, *by which cometh dissoluteness*." It is well known that the Greek particle *en*, sometimes rendered *in* in our English version is also rendered *at, by, with, among, in the presence of,* or *because of*. There is no necessity, therefore, to conceive of Paul as teaching the absurdity of moral evil being *in* the wine. He does not even say that we are not to drink it. The injunction is: "*Be not drunk*" with it.

In reference to the Hebrew term *yayin* the Reply says:

"No one can possibly show that even in one half of the texts where *yayin* occurs it has reference to an intoxicating kind of wine."

I grant that it might be difficult to convince the writer of the Reply. But the strong probability to an unsophisticated mind is, that in eight or nine cases out of every ten, the word *yayin* does signify *wine* with more or less of an intoxicating property.

Our Critic goes on to argue very fiercely against what he calls our "*prime fallacy*,"

"That whatever is the signification of a word in one text, is the signification in every other."

Here is another 'man of straw' conjured, as it would seem, expressly to show how our clever Critic can demolish it. If he has been wide awake while reading and quoting my lecture, he must know better than to suppose that I have fallen into this fallacy. I could not have expressed more clearly what our Author so laboriously strives to represent as though I had contradicted it; viz.— that the term *yayin* used to be variously applied. I quoted Dr. Eadie to show that "*yayin* was a generic name," denoting "in the *majority of instances* a fermented and intoxicating liquid," and that sometimes it seemed "to signify the growing fruit of the vineyard." I also represented that the word was used metonymically to denote *intoxication*. And yet, the Reviewer, evidently feeling that he must write something, coolly tells us about the necessity of remembering that the same word frequently connotes different things; and *stoops* to a *special illustration*, which turns out to be a very windy one, and then our Philosopher seems satisfied that he has ventilated the whole matter. But he might, if he had chosen to do so, have taken his special illustration from my own lecture with regard to the very word which he wanted to represent as meaning different things. Having previously shown the significations of *yayin* as *wine;* in some cases, the effect of drinking wine, or *intoxication;* sometimes, *the growing fruit of the Vineyard;* on p. 24, I make the following statements: "It is not necessary to prove that the term was never employed to denote the unfermented fruit of the grape. *It might have been so employed sometimes.* But it is altogether *inadmissable* to suppose that, in the case of the Nazarite who had fulfilled his vow, the term must be taken to signify *only that which did not intoxicate.*" And these words are partially quoted further on in the Reply; though only in such a manner, of course, as to suit the purposes of our Critic. All this displays a surprising cleverness in spinning out the length of a four-penny pamphlet, in which there is an abundance of quotation and abuse, but not a single solid argument against my lecture.

But it is in the matter of the law pertaining to Priests and Nazarites, that our Critic seems to meet with his '*prime*' difficulty. After quoting what I say at the commencement of the fourth paragraph in the lecture, he makes a long but very unsuccessful attempt to dispose of a very stubborn fact. The quotation from me is as follows: "The same word *yayin* is used both in the law pertaining to the Priesthood, and in that of the Nazarites." With a seeming contempt for facts, our Critic then asks:

"What of that?"

And proceeds with great resoluteness to draw his sword that he may cut in twain this "*philological knot.*"

"The sameness of the word does not abolish the difference of quality, character, and kind. Dog in the Isle of Skye may suggest a peculiar terrier; yet dog, as used in Finmark or Newfoundland, will not argue the same species of thing......... Words are always growing, or narrowing, in what logicians call their *comprehension.*"

Now, I suppose, almost any School-boy, who has learned his spelling book with much advantage, could have enlightened us with regard to this, as much as our learned Critic. But how does this interfere with the fact which I have stated? Are we really to be told that, in the law for Priests and Nazarites regarding wine, it matters not what may be the Hebrew word which is employed? It is evidently inconvenient for our Critic's position, to know, that, in each case referred to it is the same word which, according to indisputable authority, signifies *wine*. It may be equally inconvenient for him to know that the *yayin* of the Hebrews, the *oinos* of the Greeks, the *vinum* of the Latins, and the *vin* or *wein* of our own times, cannot, by any stretch of the imagination, be supposed to have varied very much from what is denoted or connoted by our own English word *wine*. From the time of Noah downwards, it has signified with a comparatively small variation, as now apparent, *intoxicating wine*. "Whatever," says Dr. Eadie, "be the precise meaning of several Hebrew terms rendered, and perhaps erroneously, by wine, the liquor commonly known by that appellation was unquestionably an intoxicating drink." And he adds very properly that "the severe denunciations against intemperance which abound in Scripture, imply the use and prevalence of an inebriating beverage."

But let it be granted, what nobody will dispute, that words are generally "growing, or narrowing, in their comprehension;" what does our Critic gain by this admission with regard to the term *yayin* among the Jews? We are not now referring to people that lived far apart from one another, as the inhabitants of the Isle of Skye, and those of Finmark or Newfoundland. The law was given to the Israelites when they were encamped together in the wilderness, and it was delivered by the mouth and by the writings of one lawgiver, Moses. That law forbade to the Priests the use of wine when they went into the tabernacle. The meaning is, I presume, that they were not to take *any kind* of wine at the time which is specified. But is there any prohibition of wine for the Priests extending to any other time? Then, with regard to the Nazarites; our Critic cannot surely expect that there will be a growing, and narrowing, of the comprehension of words, in the same chapter, and in the utterance of the same individual and the same law! If he does; then what shall be said of the tortuousness, or, if he prefers it so, the growing, or narrowing, of our Critic's own comprehension? If in Num. vi. it is said at the 3rd ver.: the Nazarite "shall separate himself from wine;" must we suppose, to please the Writer of the Reply, that wine signifies one thing in the 3rd ver., and another in the 20th? It certainly is something, although our Replier would wish to make nothing of it, that in each of the verses now quoted from, the word *yayin* is used: and it is used in such a way as not to admit of any one, with the slightest appearance of honesty, escaping from the conclusion, that the Nazarite was equally *forbidden* the use of any kind of wine during the time of his vow, and *permitted* by the express sanction of the law to *use* it after the fulfilment of that vow. We know very well that the Nazarite was not bound to take the wine because the permission was given that *he might* take it. It would be for his credit and advantage, probably, not to take it. But this is not so much the plain teaching of the Bible as the harmonious declaration of reason and experience.

After more than a page full of pedantry about the different sig-significations of words, our learned Critic quotes the late Hugh Miller as an authority for cutting the Gordian knot, which, after all his previous philosophizing, he finds that he cannot untie.

"Hugh Miller, in speaking of a doubtful philological opinion, says:—"I would, in any such case, at once, and without hesitation, cut the philological knot, by determining that *that philology cannot be sound* which would commit the Scriptures to a science that cannot be true."

Do not the words here in italics, which are our Critic's own, manifest a most murderous intent? May we not advise our hero, before he strikes at the philology of the Sacred Scriptures, to put away his false philosophy; which, in representing some physical substances as absolutely unclean and injurious, throws as much contumely upon Nature, and upon the God of Nature, as it does upon the Bible: and as much contempt upon the demonstrations of the most enlightened science, as upon all three besides. Most firmly do I believe, that there can be no real discrepancy between a true religion from God and the book of Nature. What one teaches, the other cannot contradict. There must be perfect harmony between the two books. To suppose a contradiction between them would be to suppose that God can contradict Himself. The Bible is from God. Nature is from God. And to a considerable extent, they both endorse the same great lessons. But let Dr. Lees beware of saying that they *plainly teach*, in all respects, the same thing. We can deduce from Nature and Science the laws of the planetary system. But our unaided reason could never deduce them from the Bible. It is sufficient to say that the Bible did not contradict Sir Isaac Newton! and that that philosopher neither cut philological knots in the Bible, nor contradicted its plain statements. But as he reverently took the Scriptures, he perceived that they were designed to teach lessons upon which Nature might remain for ever silent. God has mercifully given us reason in the soul, as well as the *Logos* in the book; and He requires us to go on developing the wondrous principles which reason may be eternally permitted to unravel from the past secrets of Nature. Hence He has not plainly told us in the Bible everything which the human mind may be inquisitive to know; nor has He written therein all the minutiæ of those laws by which human philanthropy may accomplish its God-like mission. Reason as well as Faith must be called into constant exercise. May the time soon come when both shall invariably exercise their functions in holiest partnership with Charity!

After quoting Hugh Miller, our Critic continues as follows:—

"In the case of the Bibbler's philology, we have only to reject a preposterous assumption, and all conflict between the demonstrated physiology of Teetotalism and the Bible at once ceases."

All this is beautifully vague and ambiguous. In the first place let us ask: What is meant by the *Bibbler's philology?* On Philology, the Penny Cyclopædia says: "It is difficult to attach a precise meaning to this word, as it is used in different significations by different writers. . . . . . Some modern writers have included, under the term philology, the study of Greek and Roman antiquities, but the majority of writers appear to regard the study of the theory of languages in general as the only subjects strictly belonging to philology." But who shall explain what our Critic means by the Bibbler's philology?

Secondly. What is the preposterous assumption that he complains of? Is it that where the Hebrew word for wine is used, it really means wine? Perhaps our Replier wishes to believe that when permission is given to the Nazarite, or the worshipper at the temple, as in Deut. xiv. 26, to drink wine, or where the priests are commanded to bring wine as a drink offering before God (Ex. xxix. 40), in these passages we must understand the word *yayin* to mean only *unfermented grape juice*, and that in other parts it signifies something stronger. But how are we to be convinced that this assumption is a true one? Our Critic will tell us that "alcohol is a *bad article*, not 'a good creature.' But this I do not believe. There are not many intelligent Teetotallers who will believe it. And no Physician in the country will affirm that alcohol is not useful for some purposes. At the same time it must be observed, that scientific testimonies of the most sterling worth unite to condemn the frequent and habitual use of alcoholic drinks. Most certainly the Word of God renders no shadow of encouragement to such a habit. And I herewith offer our Critic, whoever he be, a reward of £100 if he can verify the charge of my being a Bibbler, even in the low sense of tasting frequently and habitually any kind of intoxicating drink. I believe it is most important to be borne in mind, that what is called the moderate and habitual use of intoxicating liquor frequently undermines the constitution, and as Dr. John James, of America, has stated, "No quantity of spirituous liquors, however small, can with safety be taken daily, much less several times a day with impunity." And for the sake of economy, example, health, intellect, morality, and religion, I feel it my duty to refrain in general from the use of those liquors.

In the foregoing quotation from the Reply we have another bombastic flourish in the words: "demonstrated physiology of Teetotalism." It might have been as well if our Critic had given us less sound and more of sober explanation. The whole of the sentence is splendidly grandiloquous. But alas for our Critic's argument! Ignis-fatuus like, it is lost in perpetual mist. It may be safer to stand on good ground than press too hard after our Replier. One thing is clear even amidst the uncertain fog with which he is enveloped: he gives up the point of Teetotalism being "plainly taught in the Bible," quite as often as he maintains it. The whole affair, which was said to be "plain teaching," turns out to be a "*philological knot*," and is wrapped up in inextricable difficulty; and our heroic Defender of this *plain teaching* girds to himself the sword of Alexander, and with a force, which will astonish Biblical Critics all over the world, splits the meaning of *yayin* into two halves: the one—Alcoholic, accursed, and very pernicious; the other,— non-alcoholic juice, syrup, or paste, which is most agreeable and exhilarating. It may seem almost strange that the Nazarite might not take even the latter kind, if the distinction were so clearly marked between the Alcoholic wine and the non-alcoholic as has been supposed. But where do we find the distinction thus marked? Not in the Bible; but in Dr. Lees' philosophy. Some, however, who will not be disposed to accept the Doctor's philology, or his so-called "physiology," will stick by the teachings of the Bible, as furnishing a plain warrant for adopting any legitimate plan for saving men from ruin. Teetotalism is a plan, the necessity of which is plainly demonstrated by the abuses and experiences of every day life: and in cases where the condition of people's health will admit, the practice of total abstinence is on every account commendable.

I observe in my lecture (p. 22) that what is "called teetotal wine, which cannot intoxicate, and which does not contain a single particle of Alcohol, I have never yet seen, nor have I heard what appears to me any very particular and authentic accounts concerning it." It is well known that there is a class of light wines which are frequently called teetotal wines, and which are sometimes taken by Teetotallers, but which to some extent are Alcoholic. They are undoubtedly much less intoxicating than our strong brandied wines; but it is evident that they are not entirely free from the element which our Replier condemns as a bad article: and it was partly to remove the misapprehension, under which some persons seem to labour, that these wines are not Alcoholic, that I gave utterance to the sentence just quoted. It must be admitted that Dr. Lees' enquiries, with regard to the nature of ancient wines, and the mode of their preparation, are well worth the attention of those who are curious on the matter. But it is not to be overlooked that there is a conviction widely entertained, and shared by many of the most enlightened scholars of the day, that the cases have been comparatively rare in which grape-juice has been drunk as a beverage before the process of fermentation has commenced. Many of the Greek and Roman classics speak of the drinking of the grape juice. But any one who is acquainted with their writings must know, that what was commonly spoken of by these as the juice of the grape was nothing more nor less than wine upon which the Greeks and Romans frequently became intoxicated.* To borrow an illustration from Horace, we may refer to Lib. 1. Car. 20, where the Poet says to his friend and patron Maecenas as follows:—

> "Caecubam et prelo domitam Caleno
> Tu bibes uvam : mea nec Falernae
> Temperant vites, neque Formiani
>   Pocula colles."

"Thou drinkest the Caecuban grape, and what is broken at the Calenian press: but neither the Falernian vines, nor the Formian hills prepare my liquors." But was the Caecuban grape-juice unintoxicating? Yes, when the grape was first broken, but not when it came to the table of Maecenas. Galen describes the Caecuban as a "generous, durable wine, but *apt to affect the head, and ripening after a long term of years.*"

The following from Becker's 'Gallus' may illustrate what was frequently spoken of as "juice of the grape." The extract is from a description in the time of Augustus. "Boys, wearing green garlands, then brought in two well gypsumed *amphorae*, the time corroded necks of which well accorded with the inscription,

---

* A writer in the *Bibliotheca Sacra* has contributed the following.—"Among the uses of the grape which we have not enumerated, is that of pressing the juice from the fresh ripe clusters into vessels to be drank immediately. All persons deny that any such prevailing custom exists, although it is admitted that it is sometimes done for amusement and variety, and for the children of a family. However, no evidence that I have seen appealed to, of the usages of antiquity would seem to be sufficient to lead us to suppose that it was ever a standing usage. We cannot affirm that the butler of Pharaoh was ever in the habit of performing such an operation. He performed it in a dream, but when he was set at liberty, we simply read that 'he gave the cup into Pharaoh's hand.' (Gen. xl. 21.) Nor does the language of Greek or Roman poets, when describing the luxury of drinking the 'blood of the grape' from its fresh clusters, when treated by the rules of ordinary criticism, imply that the voluptuaries of those days were satisfied with any such abstemiousness."

whereon might be read written in ancient characters, the words, *Lucio Opimo Cos.* 'It is Falernian, my friends,' said the host, 'and is, as you know, usually clouded.' 'Actually,' said one of the guests, 'only five years more, and this noble juice would have witnessed a century pass away, and during this century there has never been a growth like it.'" And the usage of the moderns follows that of the ancient writers in respect of the term 'grape-juice.' Professor Anthon in his notes on Horace Lib. i. Car. 18, has the following. "Amid the praises, which he bestows on the juice of the grape, the bard does not forget to inculcate a useful lesson as to moderation in wine." What is here meant by "the juice of the grape" is easily gathered from the Ode to which the Professor is referring. There can be no question that Horace there wrote of wine, which was fermented, and very potent. In the course of our reading among classical authors, we may find plenty of references to all kinds of wines: but it is very seldom that we come upon a description of unfermented and unintoxicating wines. There can be no doubt that the wines used by the ancients were much weaker than the strong wines which are now used in England, and that they were accustomed to dilute their wines with water. Yet we know that a very frequent effect of their drinking habits was that they became intoxicated.

It cannot be denied, however, that the juice of the grape may be preserved without fermentation. The following statement from Liebig is sufficient to set this at rest. "If a flask," he says, "be filled with grape-juice, and made air tight, and then kept for a few hours in boiling water, or until the contained grape-juice has become throughout heated to the boiling point, the minute amount of oxygen contained in the air which entered the flask with the grape-juice, becomes absorbed during the operation, by the constituents of the juice, and thus the cause of perturbation is removed. The liquor does not now ferment, but remains perfectly sweet until the flask is again opened, and its contents brought into contact with the air. From this moment the same alteration begins to manifest itself which fresh juice undergoes; after the lapse of a few hours, the contents of the flask are in full fermentation; and this state may be again interrupted and suspended as at first, by repeating the boiling." But it is questionable if such a process as this was ever very generally resorted to among ancient nations.

They sometimes adopted the practice of straining or filtering their wines. "The wine-strainers of the Romans," says Professor Anthon, "were made of linen, placed around a frame-work of osiers, shaped like an inverted cone. In consequence of the various solid or viscous ingredients which the ancients added to their wines, frequent straining became necessary to prevent inspissation." Archdeacon Jeffreys quotes from the Delphin edition of the Classics a note, which he gives as follows. "The ancients strained and defecated their *must* repeatedly through the filter before it could have fermented, and, by this process taking away the fæces that increased and nourished the strength of wines, they rendered them weaker, sweeter, lighter, and more pleasant to drink." Pliny has been frequently quoted to show that the ancients were accustomed to break the strength of their wines by the strainer. His words are: "Utilissimum vinum omnibus sacco viribus fractis." "The most useful wine is that, whose strength is all broken by the strainer." Again he says, "Inveterari vina saccisque castrari." "Wines are rendered old and weakened by the strainers." In speaking of the *saccus*, which was the filter or strainer used among the Romans, Pliny must have referred to what is described in the foregoing note by Anthon. But there is nothing in the words of Pliny to prove that these wines were absolutely unfermented and unalcoholic. What we should naturally gather from the writer is no more than that the most useful wine was thinned or weakened by straining.

Dr. Ure, it is said, states that "gluten, being an insoluble substance, may be separated by its subsiding, or still better, by the *filter*, and that, if it be totally separated, the vinous fermentation is impossible." But have we any proof that the ancients did frequently, or sometimes, so filter the grape-juice as entirely to prevent fermentation? I will not say that they did not: but where is the proof that they did? Henderson in his history of Ancient and Modern Wines says, that a common division of wines among the Greeks was into "*polyphoroi* (bearing much), or strong wines, which would bear a large admixture of water, and *oligophoroi* (bearing little), or weak wines, which admitted of only a slight addition." Among the stronger wines of the Romans might be ranked the Faustian, and Falernian: among the weaker the Lesbian, the Mareotic, and perhaps also the Albanian. Horace writes of the Lesbian as being an innocent wine: but this does not prove that it was absolutely free from Alcohol. The Mareotic was so called from its being produced on the borders of Lake Mareotis, in Egypt. It is described as a "light, sweetish, white wine, of easy digestion, and not apt to affect the head." Yet, strange as it may appear, Horace speaks of this innocent wine (lib. i. car. 37) in these words: "Mentemque lymphatam Mareotico:"—"the mind maddened with Mareotic wine." The Albanian was said by Pliny to be very sweet or pleasant *(praedulcis)*. In the time of Horace, it was considered by Epicures one of the choicest wines known: but this does not prove by any means that it was entirely unalcoholic.

The Author of *Anti-Bacchus* gives Cato's recipe for making "vinum familiæ," family wine, as follows. "Put eighty gallons of *must* into a vessel, and sixteen gallons of sharp vinegar; pour into the vessel at the same time sixteen gallons of sapa (wine boiled down to about a third) and four hundred gallons of pure water; let these be well mixed for five days successively; to these ingredients add eight gallons of old sea-water; put the cover on the vessel, and close it up firmly for ten days. This wine will keep until the solstice of the following year, and if any of it remain after that period it will be very acid* and very beautiful." Mr. Parsons reminds his readers that "this could not be a strong Alcoholic wine." Certainly it could not: but was it Alcoholic in any sense? If it were, it was not a genuine Teetotal beverage.

Pliny has informed us that the Romans had no less than one hundred and ninety five varieties of wines, and that a sub-division of these general varieties into their separate species would number as many more. We cannot doubt, therefore, that there was a great difference in the strength, as well as the flavour of their wines. In all wine-producing countries, the peasantry would

---
* What is the acid which is here referred to? Is it the acetic? If so, does it not prove that, previously to "the solstice of the following year," alcohol must have been contained?

naturally drink, at the time of grape-gathering, the pure juice of the vine. But it is well known that as soon as the grape is broken, and the juice is exposed to a temperature of 70°, it begins immediately to ferment, even without the addition of any substance to promote such fermentation. The temperature, therefore, must be comparatively low for grape-growing countries, to admit of the peasant drinking his wine in the day-time unfermented. In Brande's Manual of Chemistry, (vol. ii, p. 1640) it is said: "Gay Lussac found that even a momentary exposure of bruised grapes to air confers on them the capability of fermenting:" that is, of fermenting as soon as they are exposed to a temperature of 70°. "Contact of air is unnecessary, and sometimes even injurious, during the progress of fermentation." Ibid. p. 1647. "Grape-juice expressed in an atmosphere of Hydrogen or Carbonic-acid may be kept for months, if excluded from air or oxygen, but the admission of a few bubbles of either of these latter, causes fermentation presently to commence, and it goes on if it once begins." Ibid. p. 1649.

There is some reason to believe, then, that wine, or liquid formed by the juice of the grape, has usually been more or less intoxicating. No one, who knows anything of ancient history, will suppose that "the term '*wine*' must always denote a liquor similar to the highly brandied port, sherry, etc. of modern times." Plutarch, as quoted both by Archdeacon Jeffreys, and the Author of *Anti-Bacchus*, sufficiently proves that very weak wines were in his time generally used and much esteemed. "Wine," he says, "is rendered old or feeble in strength when it is frequently filtered. By this percolation through the filter, the strength of the wine is taken away without any injury to its pleasing flavour, and the spirit being thus excluded, the wine neither inflames the head, nor infects the mind and the passions." If this be claimed as a Teetotal wine, be it so. But Plutarch *himself might not have been aware* that the last particle of Alcohol had evaporated, before the wine was reckoned fit for use.

It cannot be denied that wines might have been sometimes preserved by means of anti-septics. Mr. Parsons in his *Anti-Bacchus* has informed us that the ancients put a "quantity of gypsum, or sulphate of lime, into their wines. The interior and exterior of their casks," he says, "were in many cases, covered with gypsum." That the vessels, in which their choicest wines were preserved, were frequently covered and sealed with gypsum, or some kind of cement, is well known: but it is evident that, among the Romans, vessels, which were so coated, often contained fermented and intoxicating wines. "When the wine-vessels were filled," says Anthon, "and the disturbance of the liquor had subsided, the covers or stoppers were secured with plaster, or a coating of pitch mixed with the ashes of the vine, so as to exclude all communication with the external air. After this, the wines were mellowed by the application of smoke, which was prevented, by the ample coating of pitch or plaster on the wine vessel, from penetrating so far as to vitiate the genuine taste of the liquor."

It is urged that there was another method of preserving the juice of the grape; that is, by inspissation. Columella, Pliny, and Plutarch speak of it as having been concentrated into a thick syrup. In Donovan's *Domestic Economy*, it is observed, that "when sweet juices are boiled down to a thick consistence, they not only do not ferment in that state, but are not easily brought into fermentation when diluted with as much water as they had lost in the evaporation, or even with the very water that had exhaled from them. Thus sundry sweet liquors are preserved for a length of time by boiling. From these considerations it is probable, that the qualities for which the Romans and Greeks valued their wine were very different from those sought after in the present day; and that they contained much saccharine matter and little Alcohol." Archdeacon Jeffreys in discoursing upon the *sapa* and *defrutum* of the Romans says, "The truth is, these wines were rich aromatic *preserves*, containing the delicious flavour of the grape in the very highest perfection, and when drunk they were diluted with eight, ten, or twelve parts of water, according to the thirst of the drinker, and his object at the time. This large quantity of water was necessary when they were used, because they were so thick with the native sugar of the grape, and intensely sweet. The Turks and Arabs use these very wines in the present day, and modern travellers state, that they are so thick with sugar, that they are constantly drying up during their journeys through the desert, and that their leathern bottles' are made capable of being turned inside out, in order to get access with the knife, to scrape off the wine." But the question naturally occurs; is the word *wine* really applicable to syrups, jellies, preserves, and even pastes? If it be; then, of course, we know plenty about unintoxicating wines. But the very fact of the Turks using those preserves which are spoken of by the Archdeacon, is sufficient evidence that they, at least, do not regard them as wines: for the sin of wine-drinking among Mahomedans is as much a religious offence, and a crime, as any of which they can be guilty.

If there be such a thing as unfermented wine in existence, and if it has been, at any time, or is now, in general use, it might be satisfactory to many persons, to have the evidence of all this more clearly established. But on my remarking that I have not heard any particular and authentic account of it, our Critic, with his usual urbanity, breaks forth as follows:

"This is an appeal *from* ignorance *to* ignorance, and what can we say? True, it is no later than the 23rd of December, 1858, that we opened, and exhibited in a public meeting at Birmingham, a bottle of Italian wine (vino-cotto) made nearly twenty years ago in Florence by M. Peppini, which was as pure and unalcoholic as the day it was bottled,—true, we have published in tracts, pamphlets, and volumes, during the last twenty years, scores of 'particular and authentic accounts' of various kinds of pure unalcoholic wine, with the very recipes for making it, ranging from the time of Cato and Columella to the days of Fabbroni and Liebig,—but, alas! the light has not penetrated the cranial opacities of Great Harwood! Think of a man who prefers to worship idols in the dark den of prejudice, shouting to the world through a crack, that he *has never seen the sun*, and has doubts about its authenticity!"

The Replier has italicized the words, "*has never seen the sun*," and truly they ought to be rendered emphatic: for, when taken with what forms the main body of the paragraph, they beautifully illustrate the lines already quoted:

"And then, exulting in his taper, cries,
Behold the sun! and, Indian-like, adore!"

It seems to be true that our Critic on the 23rd of December, 1858, did at a public meeting in Birmingham exhibit a bottle of Italian wine. Possibly it was vinegar: and if so, this may in some measure account for his own subsequent acidity. But it is perfectly true that I was not at that time in Birmingham to witness such an exhibition. It is also true, if our Critic be the gentleman whom I suppose him to be, that I have not heard him lecture, either there, or anywhere else; nor have I read all his tracts, pamphlets, and volumes; and therefore he may suppose that I must be very much in the dark. He seems sufficiently satisfied, however, with the great amount of learning embodied in his own writings; and it may be quite true that they form a very brilliant collection. I am sure they must, if written in the style of the Reply.

But it is a cruel cut to the Harwood Teetotallers to talk of an appeal from my ignorance to theirs. And this is as thoughtless as it is cruel on the part of our Replier; for, just before my words were uttered, which are now so politely criticized, Dr. Lees himself had exhibited in Harwood the very sunshine of his own presence; and after many or most of my hearers had attended to his instructions, by what authority does our Critic speak of my words as an appeal from ignorance *to* ignorance? Moreover I would plead, that if Dr. Lees had not been here at all, there is in the neighbourhood of Harwood, and among those who heard and approved of my lecture, a power of intellect, and an extent of learning, to which our anonymous Critic will not lay any claim. Nevertheless, he is quite lugubrious over our darkness in this part of the world. "Alas!" he cries, "the light has not penetrated the cranial opacities of Great Harwood!" A writer in the *Times* newspaper has rightly observed that "there is a proverb about playing with edged tools, which is apt to present itself, when one hears of anything particularly clever or audacious." And it may not be amiss for some one to tell our Critic that the compliments, which he heaps on his *friends* in Harwood, form a kind of recompense for their patronage, which they may not, in all cases, be disposed to relish.

While speaking of the sun and the light, and the cranial opacities of Great Harwood, our Critic may have emulated the fame of a very cynical philosopher, of whom it is reported that he went to live at a place called Cranium in the suburbs of Corinth, and bade Alexander to stand out of his sunshine. We have already obtained an insight into the amiable instincts of our learned scribe: but if he will be content to come out here as a missionary, and if, like Diogenes, he will inform the world who he is, he may then say to the craniums of Great Harwood, *Let there be sunshine.* In that case, even the worshipper of idols may be found to cast away his old idolatry, and the very den of prejudice be broken open, and the authenticity of *vinegar*, or *vino-cotto*, be for ever established at the very mouth of the tub.

On p. 8 of the Reply, we observe the following.

> "He has managed to fancy that he knows something at least about *tirosh*—viz. that it sometimes signifies *mustum*, or grape-juice........Now, we ask, is 'grape-juice' wine or not?"

Perhaps it is: and like the new-wine of self-conceit, it may be apt sometimes to affect the brain. It is true that I know but little about the *tirosh* of the Hebrews, and I "manage to fancy" that our fanciful Critic knows just as little as I know about it. But to borrow the expression which he himself uses on p. 11 of the Reply: 'A *little* learning is a dangerous thing.'

It will not be questioned that pure grape-juice has been sometimes drunk at a temperature below what is necessary to fermentation, and before any Alcohol has been generated. We should usually speak of such juice as *must* or new-wine. My reference in the lecture was to a liquid wine which might be kept free from fermentation, and come into general use as a pleasant and wholesome beverage. Now if our Critic can do no more than direct us to the *must*, which will either run into a state of fermentation as soon as it is exposed to the temperature of 68° or 70°, or else become vapid and useless, he does not point out what is desiderated as a common teetotal wine, and confirms the impression, that what is bought and sold as such is more or less Alcoholic and intoxicating.

The Replier continues:

> "Does he accept the version, or quarrel with it? It is the same in other translations. In the German and Dutch it is *most*; in Italian, *mosto*; in the French, *moût* and *vin-doux*."

That is to say, it is anything in all these translations but *wine*. For the German and Dutch *most*, the Italian *mosto*, and the French *moût* and *vin-doux*, all signify *must*, before it is converted into what is commonly known as wine. But I have no desire to quarrel with our English version. Upon the whole, it is a very good one; although our Replier himself has laboured to prove that it is not quite perfect. Perhaps there are but few Hebrew scholars who would now care to translate *tirosh* by our English word *wine*. Those who have translated the Scriptures into Continental languages have doubtless displayed much judgment in the rendering which they have given. And *tirosh* might be translated, it may be, in our own tongue, by the terms *fruit*, *grapes*, or *grape-juice*, more correctly than by the word wine.

"Now if it is 'wine' at all, then, inevitably, it is yayin; i.e. a species of it; just as certainly as muffin, or, loaf, or cake, or crumpet, is a species of bread. Here then, unless Mr. W. will eat his own admissions, and contradict plain fact he *does* know something about unfermented wine." (p. 8.)

The inevitableness of this will not appear, perhaps, to many besides our Replier. For in the first place, it cannot be affirmed that the term *yayin* is exactly co-extensive with our English word *wine;* and it will not be inevitable to every mind that *yayin* was the genus of which *tirosh* was one of the species. But *tirosh* itself has been represented as "*a generic term* signifying the produce of the vine in general, from the kernel even to the husk—and perhaps the young shoots and the tendrils—but always in its solid form." These words, I believe, are contained in the works of Dr. Lees. They are quoted from "*Tirosh lo Yayin*" or as the title is given in plain English, "*Tirosh is not Yayin.*" A little further on in the same work we find the following upon the word *tirosh*. "Although translated 'wine,' 'new wine,' and 'sweet wine,' this term appears *not to have meant wine at all*, but the general produce of the vine, in the solid form of grapes, raisins, etc." Compare with all this the argument pursued on the 8th page of the Reply.

"He knows something at least about *tirosh*—viz. that it sometimes signifies *mustum*, or grape-juice. It is the word translated wine, sweet-wine, or new-wine, in 38 places of our version. Now, we ask, is 'grape-juice' wine or not? Does he accept the version or quarrel with it? It is the same in other translations. ....Now if it is 'wine' at all, then, inevitably, it is *yayin;* i.e. a species of it."

If we unite with this the statement which is embodied in Dr. Lees' "published tracts, pamphlets, and volumes," how does it look? Here *tirosh* is made to be *yayin*: there "*tirosh* is not *yayin:*" and, adding the plus here to the minus there, we have the very innocent result: that which means nothing. Or if we take the definitions which are furnished of *tirosh* in *Tirosh lo Yayin*, and combine them with what is said here, we may read the two verdicts as follows:—

TIROSH LO YAYIN.	REPLY TO THE LECTURE, etc.
"TIROSH,—*a generic term* signifying the produce of the vine in general, from the kernel even to the husk—and perhaps *the young shoots and tendrils—but always in its solid form.*"	"*Tirosh*......it sometimes signifies *mustum* or grape-juice. It is the word translated *wine*, *sweet-wine*, or *new-wine*, in 38 places of our version. Now, we ask, is 'grape-juice' wine or not? Does he accept the version or quarrel with it? It is the same in other translations. In the German and Dutch it is *most*; in Italian, *mosto*; in the French, *moût* and *vin-doux*; in the Greek version, *oinos* and *oinos-neos*. Now if it is 'wine' at all, then, inevitably, it is *yayin*."
"TIROSH. Altho' translated 'wine,' 'new wine,' and 'sweet wine,' this term appears not to have meant wine at all, but the general produce of the vine, in the solid form of grapes, raisins, etc."	

Is it not inevitably ludicrous, for the Author of the *Reply* to be quarrelling in this way with the Author of *Tirosh lo Yayin*? Why this is even more preposterous than the fable of the Kilkenny Cats.

As for eating one's own admissions, and contradicting plain fact, I shall leave that part of the business to our Critic, who chooses to contradict Dr. Lees; and I only hope that Dr. Lees won't eat him up. It will be seen, however, on referring to what I said in my lecture respecting the *tirosh*, that I was content to quote the Hebrew Lexicons with which I was familiar, and to take the opinion of Dr. Eadie. Between these I have not yet observed any real contradiction; nor is there any great discrepancy between my quotations from them and the statements which are made by the Author of *Tirosh lo Yayin*. True, the mind of the latter "had revolted at the common reading, 'The *new wine* is found in the cluster' (Isa. lxv. 8,) as offensive to a plain understanding." But sometimes the human understanding takes offence at a very trivial matter. With a moderate amount of forbearance, it may be easy to admit the term *new-wine* as applicable to grape-juice. Certainly I have no objection to its being so applied, provided this be not dragged into a wrong precedent for calling every thing which might come under the name of *tirosh*, or *sobe*, wine. The Hebrew *tirosh* should be regarded generally, I think, as *vineyard produce, grapes,* or *grape-juice;* and *sobe,* or the Latin *sapa* and *defrutum*, as sweet syrup or vinous preserves.

But to turn from the consideration of *tirosh* to that of *yayin*. If we take the latter as nearly corresponding to our English word *wine*, we shall not perhaps be very far wrong. At any rate, we cannot find a word in our own language, which more completely, and forcibly, expresses the meaning of the Hebrew *yayin* than 'wine.' Sometimes we do apply the term loosely, as the Hebrews might have applied it. Thus we talk of a good growth of wine; or pure water might be spoken of jocosely as Adam's wine; or, if forgetful of "*Hobbe's profound observation,*" which our Replier notices at the 12th page, "that words are the counters of wise men," etc., we may sometimes tell of "vinegar" as wine, i.e. "sour wine *(oxos, vin-acer)*." *Vide Reply, p.* 9.

What is wine? "Wine," says a writer in the *Penny Cyclopædia,* "is the result of the fermentation, more or less complete, of certain saccharine fluids, either existing naturally in the juices of plants, or artificially blended together............Though Alcohol, therefore, is present in all wines, yet many other principles exist in them, the number of which, and the manner in which they are blended together, as well as their relative proportion, give to different wines their distinctive properties." The *Encyclopædia Metropolitana* tells us that *wine* is "the fermented juice of the fruit of the vine, and of other trees." In another place the same authority gives us the following: "Wine, in the customary sense, is only understood of the expressed juice of the vine-grape, *fermented and matured by keeping.*" (Encyc. Metrop.; art. Wine.) Professor Johnston, in his "Chemistry of Common Life," says, "The name of wine is usually given among us, by way of eminence, to the *fermented juice of the grape.*" "All grape wines," says this writer, "contain a notable proportion of Alcohol, or pure spirit of wine." (Vol 1, p. 319). Barclay's Dictionary has: "*Wine*, a liquor made of the juice of the grape, or any other saccharine fluid, *by fermentation.*" Wright's Dictionary gives the definition thus: "*Wine*, the fermented juice of the grape." Such also is the signification given in the Imperial Dictionary. "All spirituous products," says Professor Brande, "of fermentation are occasionally denominated wines. The term, however, is more generally limited to *fermented* grape juice." He defines *must* as "the expressed juice of the grape *before* its conversion into wine by the process of fermentation." (See Brande's Dict. of Science.) Dr. Ure adopts the same distinction between *wine* and *must*. Thus he defines *must* as "the sweet juice of the grape." "WINE," he says, "is the *fermented* juice of the grape." "In common language, the intoxicating liquor obtained from the sweet juices of fruits is called wine." (Dr. Ure's Dict. of Arts; art. Must, Wine, Distillation.) The weakest preserved wine of which I have seen any particular account is a kind of champagne which bears as low a proportion of absolute Alcohol as five per cent. (See Prof. Johnston's Chemistry of Common Life, Vol. 1, p. 320.) Possibly this is the "temperance champagne" to which our Critic alludes in the footnote, at p. 15 of the Reply. If so, it may partly account for the inebriety of language for which the Reply is remarkable throughout.

Nothing which I have seen on the wines of Scripture strikes me as being more calm and sensible than what Dr. Eadie has advanced in his Biblical Cyclopædia; and, as the Replier observes that Dr. Eadie "had the candour to adopt many of the views previously expressed by Dr. Lees," it may be agreeable to our Critic if I quote rather fully from the Doctor's article. "There has been some controversy," he says, "as to the nature and qualities of the liquor which is called wine in our Scriptures. The plain reader of the Bible will be satisfied, however, that whatever be the precise meaning of several Hebrew terms rendered, and perhaps erroneously, by wine, the liquor commonly known by that appellation was unquestionably an intoxicating drink." "Like all other countries, Canaan had wines of various strength; and a distinguished writer on Jewish Antiquities observes, 'the wines in those countries cannot easily be used without water.' Another ancient author says, that 'the wine at Aleppo resembles that of Cyprus, and is so fiery that when drunk unmixed it causes great inconvenience.'" "The Hebrews," says Dr. Eadie, "had a great variety of wines, and as great a variety of articles yielded by the vine. They had many kinds of syrups and molasses, but none of these seem to have been called wine."

Mr. Homes, Missionary at Constantinople, is quoted by the Biblical Cyclop. as follows. "All that which is now called wine in the East is as truly wine as that which is called wine in France. Whether boiled or not, whether sweet or sour, all the known wines are intoxicating. The boiling which the people of certain districts choose to give to their must, for the purpose of securing a wine that will keep better, should not be confounded with the boiling of the same must for the purpose of making sugar and molasses. In the former case it is boiled perhaps half-an-hour and not reduced one-twentieth in bulk; in the latter case it is reduced more than three fourths in quantity. And hence an 'inspissated wine' should never be confounded with inspissated grape juice. The former gives us an intoxicating liquor, and the latter a syrup or molasses.

"Travellers from northern countries unaccustomed to any product of the grape but wine, whenever they have met with some of these liquid and almost solid products of it, have spoken of them as kinds of wine, as if every liquor of grape must necessarily have that name. Thus Barry states that 'the Turks carry with them on their journeys unfermented wine,' which we have seen from our descriptions could only be some kind of grape-syrup. Dr. Duff, of Scotland, travelling in France, misleads his readers in a contrary direction by speaking of wine as mere grape juice. He speaks with delight of his having seen 'the peasants carrying along instead of milk, bowls of the pure unadulterated blood of the grape.' Now although this was wine, with his old English habits he would feel no prejudice against the use of it, whether in the form of weak claret or strong Madeira." (Bibliotheca Sacra, pp. 292, 295.)

Our Critic, if he pleases, may enter on a quarrel with all the authorities which I have now adduced as to the proper signification of the word 'wine.' But he must really excuse me if I prefer to follow them rather than Dr. Lees, and believe that the term '*wine*' is properly applicable only to the fermented juice of the grape or of some other fruits. The Missionary just quoted has affirmed, and perhaps correctly, that "in the present use of language *unfermented wine is an impossibility*." But if we turn from the word to what is signified, I should earnestly recommend our Critic to have done at once, and for ever, with receipts for making wine; and as a good Teetotal advocate to give up the practice of exhibiting *vino-cotto*, and to banish all sorts of Champagne, whether it be still or sparkling, red or white, with five or fifteen per cent of Alcohol: for, to quote the expressive words of the Reply at p. 1 in the foot note, "After all, are not both brewing and boozing the 'inventions' of Man?" What do honest Teetotallers require of wine at all as a luxury? Surely they will be better and safer without it, except when illness imperatively affirms the necessity of it: and as for Teetotal critics or advocates boasting of the variety of their wines, this may become a snare to many, who cannot immediately discern between what is Alcoholic, and non-alcoholic.

After pitying, and bewailing, and then contradicting, my ignorance about Teetotal wine, our Critic consoles himself by observing.

"Well it is to be hoped, Temperance Societies have something better to do than to instruct gentlemen who are content with ignorance."

He might have said to the Society in Great Harwood, "*For ye suffer fools gladly, seeing ye yourselves are wise.*" Perhaps he thought of a Doctor who once exposed his ignorance as to the contents of Walton's Polyglot, and drew upon himself the merited reproof of one whom he had the modesty to charge with "gross ignorance," with "literary fraud, falsehood, and forgery." "What, then, is the fact?" asks Mr. Cook. "Is this writer's assertion sustained or contradicted by an appeal to the book itself? He might as well affirm before the world, that there never was such a book as Walton's Polyglot in existence, as affirm that the Targum of Jonathan and Jerusalem are not contained in that book. ....The Targum of Jonathan, which our opponent has the effrontery to declare is not contained in this work, we find occupies a considerable portion of 390 folio pages. The Targum of Jerusalem also, which he affirms is not contained in this work, we find occupies a portion of the same 390 folio pages............Now in the face of this fact, we may ask, To whom does the charge of 'ignorance' or 'falsehood' apply? Our opponent may call himself ' the truth seeker,' but when his readers see these pages they may be tempted to suspect that his qualifications either to *seek* the truth, or *speak* the truth, are not of the highest order." (Cooke's Christian Theology, pp. 172, 173.)

In reference to the pamphlet from which the foregoing is quoted, the Biblical Review for Jan. 1848, has the following. "It appears that the Author had, in his 'Treatise on Theology,' affirmed the well-known fact, that the ancient Jews in their Targums speak of a Divine person under the name of *Memra*, or the *Word* distinct from the Father, etc.; and had referred to Walton's Polyglot, as containing the Targums of Jonathan and Jerusalem. Now this Dr. Lees, Editor of the 'Truth-seeker,' but who is clearly not given to seek the truth in Polyglots, not only denies that the doctrine in question is to be found in the Targums, but denies, even in the face of all the learned libraries in the kingdom, that the Targums themselves are to be found in the aforesaid Polyglot."

In the addendum to his pamphlet entitled, "Reply to a Critique," Mr. Cooke reproves what is even worse than contentment with ignorance, viz., such contentment combined with vituperation. "Now," he says, "there are six volumes of the Polyglot; and this writer having borrowed one volume, and run over a few passages therein, ventures to affirm that the Targums in question are not contained in any of the other five; and with this ignorance at issue, denounces his opponent as *ignorant* and *fraudulent* for maintaining a statement which he himself is now obliged to confess to be true. His apology, (that he had only examined the first volume) however, is very lame; for had he only examined the first with care, he could not have fallen into this egregious error. Had he even read but the *Prolegomena*, he would have found the Targums described there as a part of the work. Had he even read the *Preface*, he would have found it stated there that the Targums were in the work. It is evident, therefore, he had read neither the one nor the other, and yet he had the modesty to parade his knowledge of the work, and affirm that his opponent knew as little of the Polyglot as he did of Rabbinical learning in general! The public have here a specimen of his truthfulness, his careful research, and accuracy in criticism ! and no doubt will be upon their guard in future. *Vituperavit quæ ignorat.* According to his own confession, he censures that which he does not understand."

If our Critic had read all this before, he ought to have learned how to write with some degree of leniency even towards those who may differ from Dr. Lees. But let him not be wilfully ignorant that wine, properly speaking, is the fermented juice of the grape, not *must* which is unfermented; that in German and Dutch, it is *wein* and *wijn*, not *most;* in Italian, *vino*, not *mosto;* in French *vin*, not *moût* nor *vin-doux;* and that boiled *sapa* or *sabe*, if preserved as an inspissated juice or syrup, is not what we should commonly regard as wine. We call syrups and preserves by their proper names, and shall not readily depart from this usage even at the bidding of our Replier. To repeat the words of Mr. Homes: " an ' inspissated wine' should never be confounded with inspissated grape-juice. The former gives us an intoxicating liquor, and·the latter a syrup or molasses." Further, he who knows anything about " *Tirosh lo Yayin*" should know, that *tirosh* is not *yayin:* and that the author of the last named work prefers to consider *yayin* as derived from the obsolete root *yavan* or *yayan*, signifying ' to froth or foam.' " Whatever the derivation," he says, " it is a general term signifying every species of *wine made from grapes.*"

The writer of the Reply professes to be very much annoyed at my " verbalism." The word is a very innocent one. Dr. Ogilvie gives the definition of it as follows : " Something expressed orally." That which is verbal is said to be "spoken, not written, oral." The fault which our Critic wishes to condemn is, that any words are used, which would seem to invalidate Dr. Lees' argument for what is called the plain teaching. To him, words, either spoken or written, verbalism or verbs in type, are alike objectionable when having any weight against the verbalism of Dr. Lees.

"Such verbalism is more pitiable than quibbling, since a quibbler does not necessarily dupe himself." (p. 9).

Now what is this verbalism, which is more pitiable than quibbling? A statement of the fact that the same Hebrew word for wine in Num. vi. 20, is also found in Prov. xx. 1. Will our Critic say that it is not? The words which are represented as very pitiable are found in my lecture at p. 23, as follows. "*Yayin*, of which it is said the Nazarite might drink after his vow should be fulfilled. . . Look at Prov. xx. 1. 'Wine is a mocker, strong drink is raging.' We have the same word translated 'wine' in this case: it is *yayin* that is said to mock or be a mocker." Any one who is capable of reading his Hebrew Bible, or even of consulting a Hebrew Concordance, can easily be satisfied that all this is true. Who then is the quibbler that dupes himself? He who tells the truth, or he who seeks to avoid the force of it? But the statement of a fact is "verbalism!" Of course it is. And this "verbalism is more pitiable than quibbling:" which is the same thing as to say that this verbal declaration of the truth is more pitiable than an evasion of the truth by artifice. In what school has our quibbling Critic learned morality? Is it so, that a fraudulent evasion of the truth is better than the truth itself? But one who verbally speaks what is true, runs the risk, as our Critic thinks, of being duped. Well, be it so, we shall prefer the truth. But we are here reminded of what the Biblical Review once said about the Editor of the Truth-seeker having sought for truth until "blinded by its excessive light." Our Critic now seems to sail on another tack; and, perhaps, may pursue error until he is blinded with its excessive darkness. But let him be advised not to fall into the Charybdis of quibbling, through an extreme anxiety to avoid the Scylla of verbal truth.

"It is not true the Bible says—and it is a blasphemy to affirm that the Holy Spirit means,—that the Nazarite might drink that wine which is *full of mixture*, or that which is a mocker." (p. 9.)

Taking the grammar of this sentence as it is found in the Reply, we are content to give this answer.—The Bible says, respecting the time when his vow should be fulfilled: "after that the Nazarite may drink wine:" and, doubtless, the Holy Spirit meant what is said. As we have seen, the Hebrew word here is *yayin*, which is a generic name, *not* for all kinds of juices, syrups, jellies, or preserves, but for all kinds of *wine*. Very rarely, it may have been applied to substances, or liquids, which are not wine; but the plain signification of the word if we take it in its ordinary sense is *wine*. It is certainly a plain disproof of Teetotalism being taught in the Bible, that the word here used is not *asis*, the fresh juice of the grape: nor *sobe*, the inspissated juice; nor *hhamer*, which was perhaps a turbid red wine; nor *mesech*, the mixed wine; nor *shechar*, the strong drink; nor *tirosh*, the general produce of the vine; nor *shemarim*, the lees or dregs of wine; nor *hhomets*, vinegar; but simply *yayin*.

But what does our Critic mean, when he writes so very glibly about the blasphemy of affirming that the Holy Spirit intended the permission to drink this wine? In the lower part of the very same page, he himself admits that such permission was given to the released Nazarite. Here are his words.

"As to the Nazarites, they abstained from *all* kinds of wine alike, even from *tirosh;* and the permission (Num. vi. 20, after that the Nazarite may drink wine) is simply *the release from their vow*..........They *then* became as common men, subject to their common responsibility........Enough for our argument that the term should be taken to *include*, not exclude, unfermented wines." (p. 9.)

Very well! Then if our Critic's words mean anything, and if, to use his own courtly phraseology, he does not eat his own admissions, he allows, that the released Nazarite had permission to drink either the fermented or the unfermented kind; and if he admits the inspiration of the words in Num. vi. 20, he must further grant that the Holy Spirit meant what is there said: in other words, meant that the permission should be recorded for the released Nazarite to drink the grape-juice either in its fermented or unfermented state. Has our Critic himself, then, fallen into this pit of blasphemy, which he had prepared for me? Or does he mean to admit after all, that fermented or alcoholic wine is not always and necessarily a mocker? Certainly, if there be a wine which, when partaken of even in the smallest quantity, makes a man senseless and irrational, reason should forbid the use of it. There would be no necessity for inspiration to protest against that. And to affirm that the Holy Spirit should sanction the use of it would be very like madness or blasphemy. But how unfortunate it is for Dr. Lees' argument, that he cannot obtain more decisive testimony, either inspired or scientific, against the use of wine in any case.

As for the drugged wine, or "that wine which is full of mixture," it will be seen, that I have nowhere affirmed the Divine sanction for the Nazarite at any time to drink that. What I have distinctly shown is that permission was given not in favour of the *mesech*, mixed wine, but *yayin*, i.e. pure fermented grape-juice, as well as all other products of the vine. No one will plead that drugs, used with strong wines for sensual purposes, can have the sanction of the Holy Spirit; and no man has a right to impute to me, or, as I believe, to any one else, any such dogma as this. But what does our Critic himself allow with regard to the mixture of wine. On p. 13 of the Reply, he writes what, I think, he is not quite sure about, that "the wine of Wisdom was pure preserved yayin, mingled at most with water, or innocent spices." * Well, then, according to that, the wine of Wisdom was full of mixture. The Replier may tell us that this was an innocent mixture. But it may be properly asked: with what consistency can he plead for a mixture of any kind, after hurling the charge of blasphemy against the supposed affirmation that the Nazarite might drink mixed wine? I have not said that the Nazarite might drink mixed wine. And I give our Critic, who tells us how to mix the wine of Wisdom, the benefit of his own quibble, only advising him not to dupe himself by exposing himself too eagerly to his own charge of blasphemy.

If any are surprised at a seeming contrariety between the two passages, Num. vi. 20, and Prov. xx. 1, it may be observed that there is no real discord between the recorded permission to take *wine*, and the declaration that "wine is a mocker," any more than there is between the permission to use other things, and the frequent representations of the Bible as to the deceitfulness of riches. Wealth is plainly represented as a mocker. What else can we gather from Prov. xxiii. 5, than a general declaration that riches mock and deceive people? "Wilt thou set thine eyes upon that which is not? For riches certainly make themselves wings; they fly away as an eagle toward heaven." Ergo, according to our Critic's logic, wealth is a mocker, and we must not have anything to do with worldly possessions in any form, and it is a blasphemy

---

* May it not have been formed, according to the custom of many among the ancients, by the mingling of various wines?

to affirm that we should. A more sensible mode of interpretation might resolve this verse into a wholesome warning against fixing our thoughts too much upon that which is seen, to the detriment of our higher spiritual interests. The passage is something like a repetition of the saying in Psalm lxii. 10. "If riches increase, set not your heart upon them."

"In all such permissions, or hortations, there is the general, well understood limitation of 'propriety.' All but Simpletons look *through* the word to the condition or thing denoted." (p. 9.)

There can be no doubt that in all Scripture "permissions, or hortations, there is the general, well-understood limitation of propriety." But this "well-understood limitation" does not appear to be the same with everybody. And the limitation, which is assigned by our Critic, may be understood by but very few; albeit he himself seems to be very much in love with it. The question, however, for consideration is, whether the limitation which he has marked out is the plain teaching of the Bible. Must we not rather lay down the "limitation of propriety" each one for himself, and as the grand result of all our reason, experience, and observation?

Our Replier is quite right when he affirms that "all but Simpletons look through the word to the condition or thing denoted." Whence we may gather that where there is a want of judgment, there will be a habit of looking through the word to something which is *not* denoted by it, as, for example, through the word "wine" in Num. vi. 20, to something that is not properly included under that term; and through the same word in Prov. xx. 1, to something which is absolutely wicked and injurious.

To pass over the next two or three pages of the Reply, we merely observe, that the Critic displays in them the force of a will, which is evident through the whole of his performance, and which reminds us of the well known lines:

> "The will made subject to a lawless force,
> All is irregular, and out of course;
> And judgment drunk, and bribed to lose his way,
> Winks hard, and talks of darkness at noon-day."

At page 11, we fall in with the sage remark:

"A little learning is a dangerous thing."

Especially in view of our Critic's freaks and antics, we are disposed to think that sometimes it is even so. But here, as in several parts of the Reply, the Writer wishes to insinuate that I am unfamiliar with the Hebrew. He himself, *alias* Dr. Lees, presumes, of course to know all about it. Now I venture to think that I know about as much of Hebrew as Dr. Lees. At least I may affirm that it has been my study, more or less, for ten years past: there are honoured Tutors now living who can certify that I have not studied Hebrew altogether in vain: and when our clever Replier can detect any actual error in my Hebrew references, he shall be welcome to tell my fellow-townsmen and the world, that I am unfamiliar with it. Meanwhile, I should advise him to speak, and to write, no more than he knows himself; and then he will not be likely to utter falsehood.

The boast of the Reviewer in the 3rd page of the Reply was, that Dr. Lees adheres " to the plain words of the authorized version, and carefully avoids critical disquisition, founded on the original Hebrew;" and then, in a foot-note, kindly represents me as getting "lost in the catacombs of a dead language." Well then, we will keep out of the catacombs; and let us see what the plain English of our authorized version shows as to a proper interpretation of symbols. Surely this will be allowed. But here our Critic waxes very indignant again, and tells us that by not going into "the catacombs of a dead language," I fall into a "pit of blunder" which is concealed upon the surface; and this is taken as proof that " a little learning is a dangerous thing."

But what is the blunder upon which our Critic is so severe? He quotes from my lecture only partially, as follows. " If we take the expression, 'red wine'.........undoubtedly it was symbolical of the wrath of God." Had he quoted my language fully, it would have exposed the futility of his criticism. Here it is, as it was given in my lecture (p. 34). " If we take the expression 'red wine,' we find it *in our English version* in two very different connections. Undoubtedly, it was symbolical of the wrath of God," etc. It will be seen, then, that by the expression, " we find it in our English version," I had really left no room for the supposition that there was any error on my part about the original Hebrew.

It was unnecessary that we should go to the Hebrew for a perfect standard of symbology. It would be enough to show that the same symbols expressed at various times and circumstances, different ideas, and that this fact must have been understood by the translators of our English Bible. But our Critic would have us to understand that he knows Hebrew; and tells us, therefore, that in the text referred to (Isa. xxvii. 2), the word which is rendered "red wine," has got in (by mistake, and that we must not read 'hhemer,' but 'hhemed.' The fact is, however, the reading in Isa. xxvii. 2, is a doubtful one. It is well known that, although several of the ancient MSS. have 'hhemed,' signifying fruitful or pleasant, and this reading is followed by the LXX and the Chaldee versions, others have 'hhemer,' which has been understood to signify a red or turbid looking wine. But the authority for the change from *hhemer* to *hhemed* is by no means conclusive. The English version has given the benefit of the doubt in favour of *hhemer*.—And Dr. Lees does not "accept the version," but "quarrels with it."

At page 12 of the Reply, our Critic repudiates the notion that red wine is symbolical of the wrath of God. It may be no great disparagement, however, to suppose that the rendering of Ps. lxxv. 8, is sufficiently correct, and that *red wine* is there to be taken as the symbol of wrath. But if the Replier prefers to think that "*yayin hhamar*," in that verse, means, "the wine is thick or turbid," we shall not object. Still, wine is the symbol of wrath. If he thinks otherwise, let me refer him to Rev. xiv. 10, "The same shall drink of the wine of the wrath of God which is poured out without mixture." In Rev. xvi. 19, we have the words, "to give unto her the cup of the fierceness of his wrath." It is to be hoped that the writer of the Reply is not so much in love with the red wine as to except this from what was symbolical of wrath. But when I affirm that it was, he observes ·

"We don't happen to think so."

What class of opinions or principles *does* our Critic *happen* to adhere to? and for how long?

" And we may express in behalf of 'the gentleman' referred to by Mr. Williams, our astonishment at his falsely ascribing such arguments to him. On turning to Dr. Lees' lecture, we find a thesis of three pages on plain symbolic-teaching; yet neither does the word red nor the phrase red-wine, occur even once."—(p. 12.)

Your astonishment may cease, dear Sir, when you cease to ignore the truth. Dr. Lees must have understood, from information which was conveyed to him when in Harwood, that the reference in my lecture was not to Dr. Lees, but to another who had discussed with me some matters contained in a previous lecture. And very shortly after, Dr. Lees himself was present at a meeting, where a letter was read from me, stating that I had not once mentioned the Doctor's name in public, and that I had not made a single allusion to anything which he had ever said or written. To whom, then, does the charge of false ascription properly apply? To myself who ascribed nothing to Dr. Lees? or to our Critic, who affirms without any proof that I did?

"Now what is really maintained by the Teetotallers is, that *bad*-wine is the symbol of evil." p. 12. "The pure wine is a figure of blessing, the *intoxicating* wine is a symbol of punishment." p. 13.

It is but fair to protest against the presumption which palms upon Teetotallers any such erroneous statements. No shadow of evidence can be furnished in support of such declarations, except the miserable error of Dr. Lees that intoxicating wine is *bad*-wine. If this were true, why should Dr. Carpenter, and others, who are as respectable as Dr. Lees in their advocacy of Teetotalism, contend for the medicinal use of it? Is our Critic prepared to run a tilt against these excellent authorities? But Dr. Lees admits that Alcohol may be used in medicine. How then can he conclude simply on the ground of intoxicating wine being a bad article, that it alone is the symbol of punishment?

"The pure wine," however, "is a figure of blessing." Our Critic's *philology* will detect no great error, perhaps, in applying the term " pure wine" to unfermented grape-juice. Suppose then that this be understood: is this innocent grape-juice never represented as symbolical of evil? In Rev. xiv. 18, the words of the angel are recorded thus: "Thrust in thy sharp sickle, and gather the clusters of the vine of the earth; for her grapes are fully ripe." On this the Tract Society's Paragraph Bible has a note. "The *vintage*," it says, "is used in the prophetical writings as a symbol of the wrath of God, or of the destruction of the wicked." That the juice of the grape symbolizes here the very opposite of blessing is evident from the following verses, where we read: "And the angel thrust in his sickle into the earth, and gathered the vine of the earth, and cast it into the great winepress of the wrath of God. And the winepress was trodden without the city, and blood came out of the winepress, even unto the horse bridles." On this passage, Mr. Barnes, of America, observes: "The representation is, that there would be a great destruction which would be well represented by the juice flowing from a winepress."

But our Author thinks that my quotation from Thomas Scott affirms the distinction for which he contends: and by the aid of capitals, italics, and interpolation, he labours to make it appear something in his own favour. In its new dress, we have the quotation returned as follows.

"'Heavenly BLESSINGS,' says that commentator, 'ARE represented by a cup of *wholesome* exhilarating wine; but the WRATH OF GOD by a cup of wine *mingled with ingredients* of that kind which tend to *produce fear, distress, and despondency*. From THIS cup,' not the other, 'the Lord dispenses to *sinners*.'"

Our Critic would have us to believe perhaps, that the Commentator meant by *wholesome exhilarating wine*, something which was unfermented, and could never intoxicate. The readers of Scott's commentary may be surprised to learn that its author was such a thorough-going Teetotaller. But if he were of Dr. Lees' way of thinking, how is it that he does not affirm the principle of total abstinence? I am not aware that Scott advocates this principle in any of his comments. In fact he writes the very reverse of Teetotal principles. On Prov. xxxi. 6, he has the following note. "Strong drink should be administered as a cordial to those who are ready to faint through weakness, or weariness; and to cheer the spirits of the dejected, that they may be raised above the depressing sense of their poverty and misery." In his Practical Observations we find the following on the same passage. "Every creature of God is good; and strong drink, though wretchedly abused, has yet its use; but instead of wasting it in excess, they, who can afford it, should dispense it to the diseased and the wretched, that by the moderate use of it, they may be refreshed and relieved." That this Commentator made no distinction between an intoxicating, and unintoxicating wine, is evident from his comments on other passages. On Gen. ix. 20, 21, he observes: "Some have thought that wine was now first made of grapes, and that Noah, not aware of its effects, was surprised into drunkenness: but this is highly improbable; for even in the most savage tribes, the art of making intoxicating liquors is known: and though a man may plant two or three vines, for the sake of the grapes; who ever 'planted a vineyard,' except for the sake of wine?" On Gen. xlix. 12, he says of the tribe of Judah: "They would have plenty of wine for exhilarating, which would sometimes be abused in intemperance, so that their eyes would be 'red with wine.'"

But our Critic tells us that Scott "affirms the very principle mentioned by Dr. Lees," viz. "that *bad*-wine is the symbol of evil." Of course, with Dr. Lees, the "*bad*-wine" is "*intoxicating wine*."* Let us see then from Scott's commentary whether he does affirm the principle that intoxicating wine is exclusively the symbol of evil. On the passage: "I have drunk my wine with my milk: eat, O friends; drink, yea, drink abundantly, O beloved, (Cant. v. 1.) the Commentator says: "He also drank the wine and the milk; the most minute as well as the more costly oblation being acceptable to him, if it come from an upright heart. He then added an invitation to his friends and beloved people, to eat and drink abundantly. The ordinances in which they honour him, are means of communicating grace to them..........The word rendered *drink* abundantly signifies, *be inebriated*."† There can be no doubt that Scott here represents inebriating wine as the symbol of what is good. On Cant. vii. 9, the same Commentator has written as follows:—" The verse may mean that the believer, having a relish for spiritual things, discourses upon them experimentally and pathetically. This is pleasant and refreshing as the best wine. ....' The delivery of my word is like to the most excellent and pleasant wine, being both well accepted of that God in whose name it is taught, and most sweetly relished by the receivers; which is

---

* *Vide* quotations from the Reply, p. 97.
† The Hebrew word to which Scott here refers is of the same derivation as the noun which is rendered in our version, *strong drink*. But it has a less offensive signification than the Commentator here applies to it. Gesenius gives it as follows.—" 1. *to drink to the full*, Hag. i. 6. Particularly *to drink to hilarity*, Cant. v. 1. Gen. xliii. 34. 2 *To be intoxicated*." The rendering, *drink abundantly*, as it stands in the passage referred to, undoubtedly expresses the proper sense.

of such wonderful power, that it is able to put words, both of repentance and praise, into the lips of him that lies asleep in his sins.' (Bp. Hall.)—'The most generous wine, of which when we have tasted, we say, let it be sent to the best of my friends, is not more powerful to make old men brisk, or to enliven those that are at the point of death, than thy words are,' etc. (Bp. Patrick.)"

Perhaps, the gentleman, who has lately assumed the responsibility of the Reply, having declared that the Bible plainly teaches Teetotalism, and that Scott affirms his principle, may very coolly tell us hereafter that Scott meant by "the best wine," unfermented syrup, and that this was what Bishop Patrick meant by " the *most generous* wine," which is powerful enough to make old men brisk, and to enliven those that are at the point of death: and so with regard to the wine mentioned by Bishop Hall as being " of such wonderful power," etc. But if Dr. Lees has not assurance enough for all this, he may possibly admit that the two Bishops, as well as Mr. Scott, speak in these passages of a fermented and intoxicating wine as "a figure of blessing:" he may also find that they speak of such wine elsewhere as symbolical of vengeance.

Other passages show that Scott regarded intoxicating wine as the symbol of blessing. His references to the Lord's Supper are enough for this. In his notes on 1 Cor. x. 16, we have the words: "The cup of wine, which was *used in the Lord's Supper to represent spiritual blessings*." But did the Commentator suppose that this wine could never intoxicate? In the notes on Matt. xxvi. 26, 27, he calls it " the most valuable and refreshing of all cordials." Would he have written thus of unfermented grape-juice? In describing the way in which the Corinthians celebrated the Lord's Supper, Scott gives an explanation of the Greek "*methuein*" (1 Cor. xi. 21) which clearly proves that he regarded the wine which was used at the Lord's Supper as intoxicating.

But neither does the note which I quoted in my lecture affirm the principle of Dr. Lees. In that note, the Commentator does not affirm that the wine of blessing was different from that which symbolized a curse in any other respect than that the latter was "mingled with ingredients which tend to produce fear, distress, and despondency; and, if drunk to excess, horror, infatuation," etc. Mr. Scott does not condemn the wine, but he tells of the evil effects of the ingredients which were mixed with it, especially "if drunk to excess." Moreover, he does not represent this cup as exclusively the portion of the wicked. "From this cup," he says, "the Lord dispenseth as he pleaseth to sinners in this world: and even his people drink some of the wine contained in it, when chastened in his fatherly displeasure." But Scott would not regard the fatherly chastisements of the Divine hand so much a curse as a *blessing* to the favoured people. The curse he regards as symbolized by the dregs of the cup; and the distinction, which he draws, is clearly not between Alcoholic and un-alcoholic wine, but between pure wine, which, to some extent Alcoholic, would tend to exhilarate, and wine which owed its stupifying properties, not so much to the Alcohol which was contained, as to hurtful drugs which were mingled with it.

Our F.S.S.A. is anxious, I suppose, to style me, Fellow of the Simeon Stylites Association, and amuses "the Harvodians" by telling them "that Mr. Williams has dared to go the whole hog." Like a genuine quack, after reverently pronouncing the name of "Dr. Lees," in the former half of the page, no less than five times, he seems to think that "the whole hog" is a phrase sufficiently dignified to be flung at a smaller personage than *Doctor* Lees. The Author of the Reply is so magnanimous, however, as not to care about controverting my "defence of drugged wine," but will generously leave me at the top of a very absurd pillar, which he is acquainted with.

"We do not care to controvert his defence of drugged wine, but leave him, a modern Simeon Stylites, at the top of the pillar of Absurd Consistency—alone in his glory. 'Red wine, *drugged*, 'taken in a proper manner, and in a reasonable *quantity*, might have cheered the heart.'" p. 12.

The words which the Replier marks as containing a quotation from my lecture, are so arranged as to express no meaning of mine. The red wine, when drugged, I had represented as a symbol of wrath. "That same wine, when taken in a proper manner:" that is, as might naturally be supposed, *free from drugs, or spices*, of any description: "and in reasonable quantity, might," I said, "have exhilarated and cheered the heart."—See p. 37. But our accommodating Replier actually tells us himself, in the very next page of his pamphlet, that " the wine of Wisdom" might have been mingled with spices. Can he affirm that the distinction between drugs and spices is, that the former are always injurious, and the latter always beneficial.

It would seem a pity that so clever a man as our Replier should forego the honour of being himself at the top of his pillar named, " Absurd Consistency." He professes to be a Teetotal Advocate; and yet he has been publishing " *in tracts, pamphlets, and volumes*, during the last twenty years," recipes for making wine; and on the top of his favourite pillar, reared, no doubt, with very much care and trouble, he has gone through sundry gyrations to the astonishment of idolaters, imbeciles, and " sham saints," below; now vehemently denouncing a Teetotal lecturer, anon exhibiting with fond delight a bottle of Italian wine, at one time condemning the defence of drugged wine, where drugged wine was not really defended at all, and in a few sentences after, declaring that the wine of wisdom itself might have been mixed with spices. He might as well have said, " *drugged* with spices," for *to drug* is " to season with ingredients."

"If the East India Company hear of Mr. Williams, they will perhaps engage him to lecture on *Biblical* principles, in defence of the Opium traffic. Who knows?" p. 12.

This, with much besides, in the Reply, is quite remarkable in the way of argument. We could suppose that the writer had studied Whately's Logic until he was tired of it, and then laid it on the shelf, resolved to have done with such dull things as syllogisms for ever. When there is no argument for a man to defend himself with, what can he do but resort to banter, and when he has not sufficient energy left to make even a good pun, why then he can yawn, fall into a reverie, and write, "*who knows?*" Perhaps the man, whose fertile brain can reach even to a " *defence of the Opium traffic on Biblical principles*," may be immortalized as a Philosopher. " Who knows?" It may suit the promoters of the Opium traffic to issue some of Dr. Lees' placards headed, " Philosophy for the People," and advertise that the Doctor will lecture on the subject: " The Opium traffic plainly *condemned* in the Bible." For a false argument is generally most damaging to the position which it professes to defend; and if Dr. Lees, or any one else, can only divert attention from the main course of reasoning which is successfully pursued against a pernicious traffic, the promoters of it will see abundant cause to tender their hearty thanks. The Bible says nothing, either about the sale of strong drink, of opium, or of tobacco : and yet there are substantial grounds for condemning an extensive traffic in either or all of them.

In my lecture (p. 34) I had suggested that "a symbol may have two very different and even opposite meanings." Our Critic tells us that this did not occur to a gentleman, who had previously discussed some statements embodied in a previous lecture of mine; and with a refinement which is nothing novel or startling, he adds :

"And if it ever occurred to yourself, that simply shows that you are disqualified from perceiving the facts really," etc.

Just before using these words, our Critic very coolly informs his readers that he chooses to take up the consideration of matters which are "immaterial to this discussion," that he may dwell, for his own amusement, and that of other philosophers, no doubt, on the kind of capacity which is indicated in my lecture.* The whole piece, from which the last quotation is selected, is so exquisitely rich in those graces of diction, which display the character of Dr. Lees' temperance, that it would be a pity to withhold it. Coming from such a source, it decidedly confers an honour on myself as the object of so many compliments.

"Several remarks occur which, if immaterial to the discussion, may as well be curtly noticed, since they indicate the kind of capacity we have to deal with. An inquiry is made in that peculiar style which ever marks incompetency when putting a poser.
" 'Did it never occur to the gentleman that a symbol may have two different, and even opposite meanings?'
" No, indeed, it did not; and if it ever occurred to yourself, that simply shows that you are disqualified from perceiving the facts really, or from expressing them truly. How can like sensible symbols, to the same understanding, suggest unlike things? It is a contradiction; and Mr. Williams is again the victim of verbalism, confirming Hobbes' profound observation, that 'Words are the counters of wise men, but the money of Fools.'" p. 12.

* Since the commencement of what is published in the preceding pages, the following has appeared in reference to the Reply, and signed F. R. Lees: "I have no objection to take upon me the responsibilities of the tract," etc. So that for convenience' sake, we may refer to our Critic by the name through which he has become celebrated, and in which he seems to glory: that is to say, Dr. Lees.

Whether the words of our Critic are his money, or his counters, I will not affirm: but they are curiosities in their way. Are they issued fresh from the mint of "True Temperance?" But with regard to the whole of what I have now quoted, I may be allowed to observe:

1. My competency or incompetency will pass in the world just for so much as it is worth; and Dr. Lees' gratuitous judgment upon a subject, which does not properly belong to him, may be more honoured when unexpressed. Let him be thankful, if his Maker has endowed him with capacities for indulging in fair argument, rather than in a spirit of low and debasing calumny. But if our Doctor of Philosophy chooses to employ his abilities in trying to throw contempt upon those of others, I wish him all the good which he may get by such an employment.

2. Dr. Lees grants in effect all that I contended for in the words which he professes to oppose. For in the very next sentence to that which is last quoted from the Reply, he says:

"The fact is that the same general word, name, or symbolism, (symbol, I suppose, is meant) besides *denoting* a given idea, *connotes* varying attributes or relations, and so only may be used differently or oppositely."

That is to say; if the Replier intends anything to be really understood by this language; a word, name, or symbol may be used with different or opposite meanings. What more have I contended for than is here expressed for me. Of course, when we talk of words, symbols, or signs, having meanings attached to them, we do not mean to say that there is thought, or intention, *in* the symbol. The meaning is in the mind which employs it: but that meaning may be conveyed to the mind of another through the medium of the symbol: and in time that meaning may come to be constantly associated with it, and thus be said to belong to it. Nothing, however, can be more obvious, than that the same word or symbol may have various significations. Writers on symbols never seem to doubt it. Instances might be multiplied indefinitely of authors referring through the same sensible symbols to various and opposite principles. I will only mention a single case. Mr. Barnes of America in his notes on the Revelation (vi. 6), has the following: "The balance was commonly the symbol of equity and justice; but it was also sometimes the symbol of exaction and oppression, as in Hos. xii. 7, 'The balance of deceit is in his hands: he loveth to oppress.'"

With a very slight variation, the same definition may be applied to a symbol, which Hobbes has applied to a name, viz. an image, or "a word taken at pleasure to serve for a mark, which may raise in our mind a thought like to some thought we had before, and which being pronounced," expressed, or represented, "to others, may be to them a sign of what thought the speaker had, or had not before in his mind." But our Critic, as quoted above, tells us that "the same general word, name, symbolism.........connotes varying attributes or relations." He in effect affirms, therefore, that the same general word or symbol has different meanings. John Stuart Mill, who is surely as good an authority as Dr. F. R. Lees on the subject of connotative names, has the following.—"Whenever the names given to objects convey any information, that is, whenever they have properly any meaning, the meaning resides not in what they *denote*, but in what they *connote*." (Mills' Logic, vol. i. p. 43). Accepting, as we must, this statement of Mill as a correct one, we are shut up to the conclusion that symbols as well as connotative names take *their meaning* according to the "varying attributes or relations," which our Critic properly says they connote.

It may be said, that a symbol can only suggest one attribute at a time to one and the same mind. But it is equally true that the object, which is used as a symbol, may suggest at different times, or to different individuals at the same time, unlike qualities or attributes, and that on account of the varying attributes which belong to it, or the varied good or evil with which it seems to be accompanied. A man, *e.g.*, may be regarded as a symbol of any one of those attributes which properly belong to him as a man, or of those moral qualities by which he is distinguished either as a fallen or restored being. To different individuals, or at successive times to the same person, a man may appear as the incarnation of moral good or evil, and that without any change in his physical aspect; or he may be regarded as the symbol of rationality, of physical strength, of moral courage, or of kingly dominion.

But our Replier asks with an appearance of great wonderment:

"How can *like sensible symbols*, to the same understanding, suggest *unlike things?*"

This is a remarkable question from a Doctor of Philosophy. But as I have not declared what he wishes to be explained, I am not ambitious to give the required answer: perhaps he will do well to consult some Elementary Treatise on the laws of simple suggestion.

"Wine is a derider (or mocker)—it bites like a *serpent*." Now here the evil consequence suggests the *kind* of wine. (p. 12.)

Doubtless it will suggest to various minds various kinds. While to one it may suggest that which bites with drunkenness, to another, who has perused some of Dr. Lees' productions, it may suggest something else which bites with biliousness and acidity.

"For wine denotes only 'a drink expressed from grapes.'" (p. 12.)

This would be true, with the addition of the word, "fermented." But we have observed authorities enough to establish very clearly that he is "disqualified from perceiving the facts really, or from expressing them truly," who applies the term "wine" to mere unfermented grape-juice, or what is properly called *must*.

"Ferment, as used by our Lord, *connotes* the idea of 'spreading' and enlarging; but as used by Paul, it *denotes* corruption." (p. 13.)

The reference both of our Lord and his Apostle to ferment or leaven, plainly indicates that they meant *influence*, which is penetrating, all-pervading, and powerful, whether it be the influence of truth or error, of goodness or of malice and wickedness.

"Different relations or properties of an object can alone denote, or connote different things." (p. 13.)

Here we have a collocation of words invented, as it would seem, for the mere purpose of passing off a mode of Scripture interpretation which is altogether arbitrary and unwarranted. If the Replier had said: "An object connotes different attributes, etc., according to its 'different relations or properties,'" we might have believed him. But the accuracy of his statement, as now quoted, is not very apparent.

> "Water, as a flood, is an emblem of destruction, but water as a cleanser, is an emblem of purification." (p. 13.)

But water as a flood is not always an emblem of destruction. The Egyptians owe their very existence to the floods occasioned by the overflowing of the Nile. "Floods, rivers, streams, and waters," says Mr. Barnes, "are often used in the Scriptures, and especially in Isaiah, to denote plenteous Divine blessings, particularly the abundant influences of the Holy Spirit."[*] The fact is, that water has been regarded both as the means of restoring and destroying life; and hence it has become the symbol of what is invigorating and life-restoring, as well as that which causes desolation; while its cleansing properties have led to the use of it as a symbol of purification.

> "So fire, regarded in its attribute of purifying, is a symbol of Divine Love; but in its different attribute of destroying, it is a symbol of His Wrath." (p. 13.)

Fire warms, enlightens, and burns: sometimes it dazzles, and destroys. We might naturally expect, therefore, that at different times it would be regarded as the symbol of what is reviving or destructive, joyous or painful. Thus it is, that from a consideration of the well known effects of the same element, it becomes to us the recognized symbol of the most opposite results or qualities, love and wrath, purification and destruction, blessing and cursing.

> "Just so with wine. The pure 'wine' is a figure of blessing, the *intoxicating* wine (however made so) is a symbol of punishment." (p. 13.)

By "the pure wine" our Replier intends, without doubt, unfermented grape-juice, which properly speaking is not wine, but *must* or syrup; and yielding to the interpretation which is here given, it only remains that we should understand wine, properly so called, as never the figure of blessing, but always of punishment. But why does the Doctor say: "Just so with wine"? He had before been drawing his illustrations from water and fire, showing that the *same* object might, by its different attributes, "connote different things." "Just so with wine," he says: and then goes on to represent that it is *not* so with wine. He did not, because he could not, adopt

---
[*] See Barnes' Notes on Isa. xliv. 3.

two kinds of water as the symbols of punishment and purification; nor could he profess to understand two different kinds of fire as symbols of Divine Love, and Almighty Wrath. But here, under cover of the phrase "just so with wine," the Replier calls our attention to a figure of blessing which is not really wine, for wine being fermented is necessarily more or less intoxicating: "intoxicating wine," he says, "is a symbol of punishment." Why does he not adhere to his former rule? Is he dissatisfied with his own philosophy? 'Twas very decent. The Doctor needed not to drop it as if it were a hot iron when he came to the word 'wine'. We will say for him what he ought to have had the courage to say himself. "Just so with wine. Regarded in its attribute of enlivening or restoring, it is a figure of blessing; but in its different attribute of creating bewilderment and intoxication, it is a symbol of punishment."

The main fallacy which runs through the Reply is in the assumption that the Jews were ever careful to distinguish between what was Alcoholic, and what was purely unalcoholic. Science was not so far advanced among them in the times of the Old Testament writers as to lead to the detection of Alcohol as Alcohol, even where it existed. Their wines, we know, were of various degrees of strength and flavour: but where do we find the line drawn in the Scriptures between the intoxicating and unintoxicating wines? Such a line of demarcation is a fiction of Dr. Lees, a thing of pure invention, by which he would represent that Teetotalism is the plain teaching of the Bible.

Our Critic, for want of something more important to stumble over, gives a kick at the term 'symbology' which I had used.

"'Symbology', for such is the execrable word which he employs." (p. 13.)

Dr. Lees may if he likes begin a quarrel with the Dictionaries: but when he has done, I suppose we shall still follow them. I observe the word, which is objected to, just as I have written it, both in the Imperial Dictionary and in Wright's. But our Doctor, who delights in such phrases as "Pecksniffism," "putting a poser," "going the whole hog," etc., is suddenly very squeamish when he comes to this term 'symbology.'

"*Symbolon* itself is a kind of word—a mark or sign; and Logos (logy) is also a word or sign. If these kindred words are to be married (or marred) together, it should be symbol-ology—but we denounce the union as grammatical incest."

Denunciations come cheaply: and perhaps our denunciator has a few to spare for other words of the same class, such as *typology*, etc. Certainly if *typology* be a good word, the main objection which is urged against *symbology* cannot be of any worth: for the greek *typos*, as well as *symbolon*, signifies a mark or sign. But why should we not have the *logos* wedded with these forms as well as any other? There is nothing very incongruous about the literal meaning, which is conveyed by the compound; *i.e.* a discourse about marks or signs. But whatever may be Dr. Lees' feeling about it, the word *symbology* has been used by men of much greater learning and ability than either he or myself. The Doctor in his grand preciseness may be welcome to the word *symbolology* if he prefers it: but he might as well battle with the tide of old ocean as attempt to resist the inevitable tendency of words whether spoken or written to abbreviation. In a language which, like the English, contains in it the elements of a great variety of older languages, this tendency will be all the more apparent. Our Author who objects to the shortening of '*symbolology*," has no objection, it may be, to the word *city* which comes remotely from *civitas*, nor to *envy* in preference to *invidia*, nor to *Emperor* rather than *Imperator*, nor to *traitor* instead of *traditor*, nor to England, which some derive from Angle-land. Then why so very menacing about the abbreviation of symbolology? When a man is too ready to talk about an innocent word being execrable (*i.e.* worthy to be cursed), it is a sign that he is losing his good temper, if he had any before; and it is always pitiable to find an advocate of true temperance forgetting his proper dignity by snarling at a word. By the bye: can our Author give us the etymology of Teetotalism? It may be a valuable contribution to modern philology, if he can.

"In the same volume of Dr. Lees' work already cited we find a passage from a Jewish Rabbi who lived before Apostolic times, declaring that boiling the wine of the offerings *improves* it. Now, boiling would make sad work of the fermented kind." (p. 13.)

The testimony of the Jewish Rabbi is in itself no proof that the wine of the offerings was always boiled, or that it was even generally boiled. There is no reason to believe that it was. It is very possible, however, that, according to the notions of this Rabbi, the wine was improved by boiling the must which was afterwards fermented, and thus made into wine. To show how this process of boiling may have improved the wine, I will here quote again from Mr. Homes as quoted by Dr. Eadie. Speaking of the wines now made in the East, he says: "Although by boiling the must, the wine is preserved sweeter than it would otherwise be, such wines are still intoxicating, and some of them extremely so." Dr. Eadie makes use of the authority of Eli Smith, an American Missionary, in Syria, as follows. "Mr. Smith made it a point, about three years ago, to inquire into the nature of the wine manufacture in seven districts of Mount Lebanon. The results he published in the American Bibliotheca Sacra, for May, 1846. He speaks of three different processes of wine-making. Sometimes the simple juice of the grape is fermented without any previous preparation. The quantity thus made is small, and does not keep well............ Sometimes the grape juice is desiccated or *boiled down* before fermentation. The quantity made in this way is very great. The must is first separated from the skins, and the boiling is done before fermentation. The effect is to clarify the must, by causing the crude substances to rise in the form of a scum, which is removed by a skimmer. As soon as this ceases to rise, the boiling is stopped, and the must set aside for fermentation. The quantity is usually diminished only four or five per cent by boiling, and the wine is commonly sweet." *(Eadie's Bible Cyclopædia—art. Wine.)* If Dr. Lees objects that reference is here made only to the boiling of the *must*, he should remember that he himself has affirmed that "wine denotes *only* a drink expressed from grapes." Wherefore, according to his style of definition, must is wine, and the boiling of the must is all one with the boiling of the wine.

The Editor of the Bible Cyclopædia is evidently no apologist for brandied, or for drugged wines. In the article just quoted he adds: "The practice of adding to the strength of wines by the infusion of brandy is unknown in these regions (about Lebanon), and drugged wine is equally unknown. Mr. Smith, says, 'On the other hand, unintoxicating wines I have not been able to hear of. All wines, they say, will intoxicate more or less. So in regard to fermentation, when inquiring if there exists any such thing as unfermented wine, I have uniformly been met with a stare of surprise. The very idea seems to be regarded as an absurdity.'"

"Clearly, then, Teetotallers do *not* call good wine an evil thing; but they certainly do prefer the advice of the writer of the Proverbs, who reprobates some kind of wine as 'a mocker,' to the conduct of Mr. Williams, who failing rightly to discriminate the word of truth, confounds in one common category, the blessing and the bane, the wine of wisdom and the wine of wickedness." (p. 13.)

According to this, we ought to read, Prov. xx. 1, "*Some kind of wine* is a mocker." But the translators had not the benefit of Dr. Lees' criticisms, and so the passage remains: "Wine is a mocker:" and most persons may be content with the ordinary version, especially as the introduction of the words, "*some kind of* wine" would appear very much like an anti-teetotal interpolation.

But the information is needless which declares that "Teetotallers do *not* call good wine an *evil-thing*." We know that they commonly regard the *evil* as consisting in the *ordinary and habitual use* of wine. The following is extracted from an admirable little work entitled: "Alcohol: its place and power:" lately published by the Scottish Temperance League. "In certain fevers—such as typhus—there is marked and dangerous tendency to nervous depression; under which, if unchecked, the vital functions become faint, and are apt to cease. Practitioners have in consequence learnt, in certain cases, and still more in certain epidemics, to anticipate and oppose this evil, by an early and judicious use of stimulants. What! wine and brandy in fever! Most certainly. Then is the time to see the use and value of Alcohol. There is nothing in nature without its use. Scorpions, snakes, fleas, bugs, and such unpleasant and apparently unprofitable specimens of zoology, may sometimes puzzle the ordinary observer who would define their exact use in society; yet, bewildered though he be, he may rest satisfied of this, that their operations *are* beneficial, *sometimes* and *somehow*. And so of Alcohol. Often it is most noxious; and looking at the wide-spread mischief that is ever working around them, superficial observers may be tempted to think that it is only evil, and evil continually. But in this, as in other things, the saying of the wise man comes true, 'To every thing there is a season, and a time to every purpose under heaven.' While standing at the bedside of a fever case—urgent, yet doing well under wine—the ship in a terrible sea, yet obeying the helm in its every turn, and steering steadily—I have often wished to have a tippler or a drunkard on one side of me, with a 'fanatical teetotaller' on the other, in order that I might have the pleasure of saying, 'There, gentlemen, there is a glorious example of the true use of wine.' The man is taking a table-spoonful of sherry, every hour, or every two hours— or a somewhat larger allowance of claret, or a smaller proportion of brandy,—the form and dose of the Alcohol varying to meet the varying phases of the disease; and at every dose you can almost see— far more truly than you can see grass growing in a warm summer shower, after long drought—health returning to the otherwise sinking frame :—the cheek less flushed, the skin more cool, the eye more steady and clear, the pulse less frequent and more strong, the tongue more moist and clean, the breathing easier, the sensations all more comfortable. What is the Alcohol doing? Not feeding the man in reality, as one might be apt to suppose; but stimulating the nervous system; spurring the nerves and the nerve-centres, and keeping them awake, when otherwise they would go to sleep, and leave the vital functions, first to flag, and then to fail utterly—going to sleep too. The nervous power is kept active, and this excites the vital force to work also. 'But the vital strength,' you will object, 'must be soon used up in this way—exhausted.' There is a risk of that, no doubt: but better to run that risk, than let all perish at once without an effort. And by and by the stomach will be enabled to receive some food again, and to digest it too; whereby the vital strength will be sustained and replenished, so as to meet the strain. The steamship in the storm—to take up our illustration once more—has but a limited supply of coal; and a vigilant production of steam, to work the engines, as she labours in the sea, will tend ultimately to exhaustion of the store no doubt; but still the only chance of safety lies in 'cracking on,' with the hope that thereby she may be enabled to reach some friendly shelter, to both 'coal and water' for the rest of her way." (Alcohol: its place and power. pp. 29—31).

The talented author of the work now quoted, while thoroughly advocating Teetotal principles, makes no concealment of the value of good wine. But in such a case as is here referred to, it must be evident, that the wine which would prove a mocker, is the unfermented stuff called by Dr. Lees good-wine, not the fermented sherry or claret.

As to the true source of the evil which is exposed, where Solomon says, "Wine is a mocker," we may cite the evidence of a Jewish writer in the Apocryphal book of Ecclesiasticus. "Wine," says the son of Sirach, " measurably drunk, and in season, bringeth gladness of the heart, and cheerfulness of the mind. But wine drunken with excess, maketh bitterness of the mind, with brawling and quarrelling." (Ecclesiasticus, xxxi. 28, 29.)* Without attaching undue importance to the writings of the Apocrypha, we may at least regard this declaration of an ancient Jew as establishing the same point with that of the above quotation from Miller. Both serve to show that " *the evil consequence*" of wine drinking *suggests not* " the *kind* of wine," but rather the measure and the season in which it is drunk. Dr. Lees' potations from *his* wine cask may be productive of very disastrous results, if he has not judgment to drink in *proper measure*, and at the *proper time*.

But I am accused of "confounding in one common category, the blessing and the bane, the wine of wisdom and the wine of wickedness:" and all this through "failing rightly to discriminate the word of truth:" by which we must doubtless understand Dr. Lees' truth. I have looked for such an expression in our English Bible as "wine of wickedness," and I can't find it. But we find the following in Prov. iv. 17, which is a testimony concerning the wicked: "They eat the bread of wickedness." Shall we then turn round upon our Critic, and affirm that, "failing rightly to discriminate the word of truth, he confounds in one common category the blessing and the bane, the bread of wisdom and the

---

* To the same effect is the version followed by the book of Homilies, in the rendering of Isa. v. 11, "Woe be to you that rise up early, to give yourselves to drunkenness, and set all your mind so on drinking, that ye sit swilling thereat until it be night."

bread of wickedness?" According to his method of reasoning, one might observe: something is here mentioned which must not be eaten: and proceed to analyze the produce of the baker's shop to find out what is this wickedness which is bound up in the loaf. Some, perhaps, will detect it in the manifest result of an old leaven, which they may even find scriptural authority for condemning as the "leaven of malice and wickedness." But Prov. iv. 17, is not the only place where solid food might seem to be marked with the Divine disapprobation. In the same chapter which tells us that, "wine is a mocker: and whosoever is deceived thereby is not wise;" we read: "Bread of deceit (in the margin it is, *bread of lying*, or *falsehood*) is sweet to a man; but afterwards his mouth shall be filled with gravel." (Prov. xx. 17.) Now, as our Critic sagely reminds us on the eighth page of his Reply, "muffin, or loaf, or cake, or crumpet, is a species of bread." He might have said that bread is made of wheat, or barley, or oat, or rye. But who shall tell us which is the condemned article to be regarded henceforth as the bread of wickedness? The vegetarian may help us here.—'*Lechem*,' he may tell us, is the Hebrew word for bread. But it is used also for all kinds of food. It is a generic term for fruits, and vegetables, and bread made from grain, and also animal food. The word *lechem* is rendered *meat*, in Prov. xxiii. 3, where it is called "*deceitful meat*." Who shall deny then, if vegetarianism can produce such a logician as Dr. Lees, that vegetarianism is the plain teaching of the Bible? In the passages now referred to, certain articles of food are condemned as bad articles. This may be said, with at least as much semblance of truth, as that certain kinds of drink are condemned. "The advance of science has shown that animal food is injurious to the human system." So say some of our vegetarian friends. "It is the cause of a large amount of intemperance, gluttony, licentiousness, disease, poverty, lunacy, crime, and premature death. The use of it is a departure from Edenic innocence." Further, it may be argued, that in the passages just quoted from the book of Proverbs, the evil connected with the food *suggests the kind* of food. "Clearly, then, vegetarians do not call good food an evil thing; but they certainly do prefer the advice of the writer of the Proverbs, who reprobates some kind of food as food of wickedness, food of deceit, and deceitful meat, to the conduct of—(Dr. Lees?)—who, failing rightly to discriminate the word of truth, confounds in one common category, the blessing and the bane, the bread of wisdom and the bread of wickedness."

Such would seem to be a fair specimen of the logic by which Teetotalism is represented as the plain teaching of the Bible. But in consideration of the blessing and the bane, it may be seriously asked: Is not the *bane* of our country, according to Teetotal Advocates, *drunkenness?* What is the blessing which they should strive to secure, but a wise use, on the part of the people, of what is good for man in its proper season; whether that proper season be in health or in sickness? The man, who confounds the blessing and the bane, is he, who spends time, not in distinguishing between sobriety or ordinary abstinence, and drunkenness, but in censuring teachers of Religion and Teetotalism, simply because they cannot do homage to his illogical blundering; and who is ever dreaming that wine, which is valuable as a medicine, must be confounded with the improper use of it, for purposes of mere conviviality or debauchery.

On my quotation of Prov. ix. 1, 2, (p. 37) our Critic says:

"Wisdom teaches how to *boil* the wine, and the same wisdom how to mix it—not with drugs, but with water." (p. 13.)

Whose wisdom teaches all this? Clearly, Dr. Lees'. It is certainly not the teaching of the Bible: for that says nothing about the boiling of wine, nor does it tells us that we must mix it with water.

"'Who hath woe! They who go to *seek* mixed wine.' Why? Because poisonous and inflaming drugs were mixed in it for sensual purposes." (p. 13.)

One important part of the declaration, which is here quoted from the Proverbs, is overlooked. When it is asked, ch. xxiii, 29, 30, "Who hath woe," etc., the answer given is this: "They that tarry long at the wine; they that go to seek mixed wine." The whole of the passage, when taken together, proves that it was the inordinate love and *excessive drinking* of mixed wine, which led to the sensualist's misery. Our Critic would leave out of sight the *tarrying long* at the wine, as a matter of no importance. *Excessive* drinking he may regard as an evil scarcely to be thought of, in comparison with the villainy of touching, port, or madeira. But it is precisely in this *tarrying long* at the wine that men are commonly deceived by it to their ruin. "*At the last*," said Solomon, "it biteth like a serpent." We may very properly decide that it is safer not to take wine at all in the time of perfect health; and in saying so we shall not *contradict* the Scripture: for certainly that nowhere tells us that we must always take wine. But what is really condemned in the word of God is intemperance, not the sin of touching what is Alcoholic.

The writer of the Reply contends very earnestly for the teaching of Teetotalism in Prov. xxiii. 31. "Look not thou upon the wine when it is red," etc. On this passage we have the following.

"The argument of Dr. Lees was not that we must abstain from intoxicating drinks *because* they are red, or effervesce, but quite different: that the Bible plainly describes a fermented wine, and says in regard to it, '*Look not upon it,* for at last it biteth like a serpent.'" (p. 13.)

It is quite enough to say on the passage which is here referred to: it tells of *wine*: and if our Critic has a favourite *wine* which he uses as an article of luxury (especially if, according to the acknowledgment which he makes on the following page in the Reply, he has *bottles* of *red wine*), he is clearly as much prevented by this passage from looking upon that, as another is from looking upon weak table beer, which is not wine, and which has neither the colour nor properties which are here described. The line of distinction is not really drawn in this passage between what is alcoholic, and what is wholly unalcoholic. To find such a line of distinction we must rise above the plain teaching of the Bible into the cloud-land of Dr. Lees' imagination. What is clearly pointed out is a luxury called wine, a luxury upon which some in Solomon's time were too intent. Nothing at all is said about fermentation, although something is said about an eye or a bubble in the cup. The following is perhaps as exact a rendering of the Hebrew as can be given. "Look not upon the wine when it is red, when it giveth its eye in the cup,—it floweth smoothly." But what is here said about the eye or bubble in the cup is no more descriptive of a fermenting than of a slightly effervescent motion.

But our Critic will strive to maintain that in this passage it is "*the wine of the sensualist,*" which is pointed out. Of course, any wine is the wine of the sensualist when it is made use of for mere sensual gratification. On p. 13 of the Reply he tells us with a great show of confidence what this wine was.

"The wine of the sensualist was the drugged *mesech*, a bad species of *yayin*."

According to this, if the wine, in the passage which we are considering, was the wine of the sensualist, "it was the drugged *mesech*, a bad species of *yayin*." But does Dr. Lees suppose that people will receive this as a correct description of all fermented drinks, and of fermented drinks only?

Our Replier seems to think that the passage quoted from the Proverbs has no condemnation for the improper and excessive use of what is not fermented. I think it has. Let us suppose a case: —and it is by no means an impossible, or a rare one—that of an individual, who has injured himself through an extraordinary taste for some sweet syrup, or drugged preparation, and who is evidently suffering from an excessive use of that which, though it does not make him drunk, may have power enough to hurry him to an untimely grave. Should we not be justified in giving him exactly the same advice which we find in Proverbs? "Look not upon it. At the last it biteth like a serpent." It may be imagined by some that drinks which are sanctioned by Teetotallers, are never productive of much injury. But this is a mistake. The following is but one of a multitude of cases, which might be adduced in point. Todd of America, in his Student's Manual, tells us of a distinguished lawyer, who "used to congratulate himself that the only luxury in which he indulged was good coffee in the morning: to make it to his taste, it amounted to just half as much ground coffee as he drank liquid. He shone brightly while he lived, but, without any disease or sickness upon him, he sunk into the grave before the age of forty. He died worn out, and seemed an old man." It is well known that cases have frequently occurred of death by drinking vinegar. Many eminent physicians have carried on a vigorous attack on the deteriorating effects of strong tea when too often indulged in. Unquestionably with regard to any-thing and everything, which has too great a hold on the appetite, the prayer is important to be remembered: "Turn away mine eyes from beholding vanity."

In the Word of God special rules are sometimes laid down for special circumstances. The book of Proverbs abounds with such rules, many of which could never be intended for universal application, but are *wise sayings* for the regulation of mankind in peculiar conditions and circumstances. Prov. xxvi. 4, 5, are evidently such: and so are Prov. xxiii. 31, 32. The language here employed was specially addressed to young men in view of the debauchery common at their carousals. But the advice admits of broader application. The eye very often tempts the heart. By seeing we learn to love. And knowing this, the inspired writer was led to use the words which are translated, "Look not upon the wine." Epicures, both young and old, have been accustomed at different times to look admiringly upon the beauty of its colour, and to talk in company about its various properties; and it is a saying worthy of the wise, and an injunction worthy of the Divine Spirit, that is written in the words: "Look not upon it."

But I repeat, despite the charge of "imbecility" which is flung against the assertion, that the difference is not clearly marked in this passage between intoxicating and unintoxicating wines. In fact there is not expressed a single point of difference between them. That which is here said in reference to wine; keeping out of sight the name; is as applicable to Teetotal beverages, as to wines that are more or less Alcoholic. Admitted that a smaller quantity of the latter may do injury than of the former: in either case, it can only be said that by an improper and excessive use, it bites, and stings, and excites irregular desire.

"Some intoxicating drinks are not red, and some Teetotal wines are—for we have bottles of them;—but does it therefore follow that the reddening of the juice, the generation of the eye or bubble, and the turbid or fermenting motion,—are not signs of intoxicating wine?" (p. 14.)

"*The turbid or fermenting motion*" is a mode of expression which is not warranted either by our English version or the original Hebrew. Three things, however, I will readily grant. 1.—That, in the passage referred to, *wine* is mentioned. 2.—The wine is said to be of a red colour. 3.—It is said to give its eye, by which we must probably understand an effervescent motion. The description is no distinctive description at all of what is fermented, except as it is conveyed in the word *wine*. All the rest is as applicable to a reddened and effervescing teetotal beverage, which is sufficiently palatable and hurtful, as to anything that is alcoholic. But it is impossible to apply this description to everything which is fermented, and at the same time exclude what is properly called wine. And if the Replier insists that the passage is condemnatory of every species of intoxicating drink, but not of his favourite wine, may he have much enjoyment in the smiles which he provokes. The fact is, Dr. Lees has simply to make his choice between the two horns of a dilemma. Either unfermented grape-juice is wine, or not. If it be, then, in the name of conscience, as he thinks that the Bible teaches total abstinence from wine, let him give it up, and talk no more about recipes for preserving grape-juice and making wine. But if unfermented grape-juice be not wine, then wine is what it is commonly understood to be, viz.: a *fermented* juice, and *that only*, and the Doctor should honestly acknowledge that if the Old Testament says once: "Look not upon the wine:" it utters its sanction in favour of the use of wine no less than five or six times, or more than that. Once, in the law of the drink offerings connected with the service of the tabernacle. Exod. xxix. 40. Lev. xxiii. 13. Num. xv. 5, 7. Again in the case of the released Nazarite. Num. vi. 20. Again in the case of the worshippers at the temple in Jerusalem. Deut. xiv. 26. Again with regard to those that are of heavy hearts, or bitter of soul. Prov. xxxi. 6. Again in the offering of wine by the hands of Jeremiah to the sons of Jonadab. Jer. xxxv. 2. Moreover the Bible represents God Himself as the Author of "wine which maketh glad the heart of man." Psalm civ. 14, 15. In all which passages the general Hebrew word is employed, which signifies wine: i.e. *yayin*.

"These signs meant *something*, we suppose, or Solomon would not have referred to them." (p. 14.)

To which profound observation, we answer: Certainly: but who says that they did not mean something?

"But Mr. Williams argues that, because *he* does not know what they meant, they either meant nothing, or at least, did not mean 'fermentation'! (p. 14.)

Which any one who reads my lecture may know to be false: for I argue in no such manner.

"To the quibble." (p. 14.)

Always, when we have to do with quibblers.

"That we cannot regard this text as a warning against pale intoxicating drinks, because it describes only a red intoxicating drink, what shall we say?"

Say, Doctor? Say the truth: that this is a quibble of your own. Solomon only describes a kind of *wine*, and apart from the word 'wine,' or '*yayin*,' he does not employ any word in this passage which *can* be rendered intoxicating drink. And you yourself are pleased to tell us that the word '*yayin*' does *not* always denote what is fermented. The only thing in the passage, which might be supposed to indicate fermentation, is "*the eye*," or bubble, "in the cup:" for the *moving straightly*, or *flowing smoothly*, which is next referred to, cannot be said to mean fermentation and nothing else. Our Critic himself can only guess at such a meaning. But we want more than a random conjecture on which to build a solid argument. And with regard to the wine giving "its eye in the cup," possibly this may apply to our Replier's 'temperance champagne,' but to fermented liquors in which the process of fermentation is completely over, and in which there is nothing to promote an effervescent motion, the description is altogether inapplicable. The inspired writer describes a kind of wine which our Critic calls "the wine of the sensualist," and of which he says: "it was the drugged *mesech*, a bad species of *yayin*." This species, however, cannot be said to include the genus, intoxicating drink. But what of pure wine which is not drugged? Is there none such that will intoxicate? And are we bound to believe that when Solomon was describing the drugged mesech, he meant to describe what is *not* drugged?—in fact, everything which might prove hurtful, except our Doctor's favourite wine?

"We are not called to confute imbecility." (p. 14.)

True: but our Replier should at least check the too eager manifestation of his own. Is it imbecility to suppose that Solomon, even under the inspiration of the Holy One, should have been incapable of expressing himself more clearly, if he meant intoxicating drink, and that only? Could there be no *plainer teaching* to the effect that all fermented liquors must be avoided, than by the employment of words which are just as applicable to drinks *not* fermented, but *only drugged?* Are we to suppose, in reaching the level of our Critic's sanity, that the inspired writer could come no nearer to the specific difference and property of what he wanted to describe, than by going off into a general and poetic description of what is common to a variety of drinks, which are either alcoholic or un-alcoholic? In other parts, where the whole category of intoxicating drinks is referred to, the words '*yayin*' and '*shechar*' are used, denoting wine, and all kinds of strong drink. The ancient Priests and Nazarites were forbidden, at the seasons specified, to taste either *wine* or *strong drink*. There is no mistaking the intention of the law in their case. Then if it were the design of inspiration to teach that all which can intoxicate must be totally abstained from by others, how is it that neither Solomon nor any other inspired writer can be found to speak more distinctly upon the matter?

Our Philosopher intimates on the fourth page of the Reply, that I have blundered by a "*misapprehension* as to the *possibility* of the Old Testament furnishing a command for total abstinence always and for everybody." (Quotation from the Reply, p. 61.) What shall be said as to his singular consistency? There he plainly declares the *impossibility* of the Old Testament furnishing an injunction, which he here strives to represent as being *furnished* in Prov. xxiii. 31. The Doctor has really decided against this, or any passage in the Old Testament, being a precept for the practice of total abstinence. But he is so marvellously wise in his own esteem, that he pronounces the utterance of this decision by another *imbecility*. It is well that so sage a reasoner should be styled, *Doctor* of *Philosophy*.

But "these signs meant something, we suppose, or Solomon would not have referred to them." No doubt, they did mean something. Perhaps a severer temperance is here inculcated than is commonly thought of, when a man sips his sweet syrup, becomes very bilious, and his heart utters perverse things. "Yea, thou shalt be as he that lieth down in the heart of the sea, or as he that lieth upon the top of a mast. They have stricken me, shalt thou say, and I was not sick; they have beaten me, and I felt it not." "But of what avail to the man who *will* interpret language from no stand-point save his own?—who, in fact, to suit a prejudice or an appetite, would *understand the same words differently*."

"It is the same sort of morality and logic which prevail amongst the Turks of fashion. The law, say they, only prohibits 'Wine'—therefore, we may consume ('Brandy')!" (p. 14.)

With this simple difference, however, that I do not say: "We may consume brandy." I believe that nothing could be more destructive of sound health than the constant consumption of brandy. But undoubtedly, an intelligent Turk, when asked if Mohammed had distinctly proscribed brandy, would make answer: No. What other reply could he give? Would our Critic have him to say: Yes? But if the Turks of fashion have no more wisdom than to indulge in brandy, they are certainly on that account to be much pitied.

"With Mr. Williams and the Turks—Names and Accidents are every thing; principles and essences nothing." (p. 14.)

As I have the honour to be named in connection with our friends, the Turks, I can only say that we shall always be very observant of names and accidents, for the proper consideration of them is important. But we shall look very narrowly into Dr. Lees' peculiar *principles* and *essences*, before we are committed to any of them.

Our Critic intimates that the injunction, "Look not," implies another, viz., "taste not": and by way of illustration, we are favoured with the following:

"'Covet not'. Does that mean 'Steal not'? No—nevertheless, he who obeys that injunction will never steal." (p. 14.)

But here I would observe that the plain teaching of the Bible respecting honesty is not conveyed by implication merely. When it means, 'steal not,' does it merely say, 'covet not?' The eighth commandment says plainly enough, "*Thou shalt not steal.*" And this we think is a command for honesty "always and for everybody."

If Teetotalism be as Dr. Lees asserts the plain teaching of the Bible, why are we lectured on the absurdity of looking for a similar command, saying, "Thou shalt not drink wine nor strong drink." But instead of such a command, we read expressions like these. "After that the Nazarite may drink wine." Num. vi. 20. "And thou shalt bestow that money for whatsoever thy soul desireth, for oxen, or for sheep, or for wine, or for strong drink, and thou shalt eat there before the Lord thy God, and thou shalt rejoice, thou, and thine household." Deut. xiv. 26. Such are not proverbs, but plain expressions of a Divine law. Do we ask why wine was permitted? The Bible makes answer: "Wine maketh glad the heart of man": (Ps. civ. 15.) and furnishes precisely the same directions which the most approved medical science prescribes: "Give strong drink unto him that is ready to perish, and wine unto those that be of heavy hearts." Prov. xxxi. 6. In these passages there is something *plainly expressed*, not in favour of total abstinence, but in favour of the permission that the Jews might, when they saw it fit or necessary, make use of strong drink. And doubtless, both Turks and Christians will have discernment enough to see, that Dr. Lees' manufacture of principles, and essences, to suit these expressions, is an expedient for getting out of a difficulty, which, nevertheless, he cannot escape.

On my observing that "the command ('Look not thou upon the wine'), is intelligible enough to any one who does not want to make more of the text than is intended by it," our Replier says:

> "There is, we fear, no great tendency in men to find more *self-denial* in a text than it contains: the bent is quite the other way. We are disposed, therefore, to return the remark in an amended shape. 'The command is *intelligible enough* to any one who does not want to find *less* self-denial in the text than is plainly intended by it.'" (p. 14.)

Very well, Doctor: the remark is as good in that shape as in the other. But would it be attended with no self-denial, or self-mortification, in your own case, if you should be driven to confess that this passage condemns, next to the drugged *messch* of the Jews, all needless luxury and intemperance? Is it not true that in the face of this expression, "Look not upon the wine," you persist in boasting that you have bottles of red wine in your own possession, and that no later than December last, you caused people to look upon a bottle of Italian wine, by exhibiting it at a public meeting in Birmingham? Is this the way in which Dr. Lees exhibits himself as a pattern of self-denial? For myself, I may say that I am not in the habit of taking wine. But perhaps it will be conceded, that when the human system is far reduced, or life itself is imperilled, it may be the dictate of duty and common sense for a man to act upon rational advice for the recovery of his health: and Dr. Lees may be assured that it will be something very different from his authority, or his censure, which will lead me, in such a case, to despise the monitions of my own conscience, and the evident teachings of the Divine Word.

Perhaps we shall be told that Teetotalism allows the medicinal use of strong drink. On Miller's statement: " Alcohol is a medicine, powerful and often precious:" Dr. Lees observes: "It (i.e. the declaration of Miller) seems to me to *be* Teetotalism."

Undoubtedly such Teetotalism is in perfect harmony with Solomon's advice: "Look not upon the wine": but it is evidently not taught in that passage.

We have next in the Reply a delicious piece of criticism on the Greek word, *scopeo*, and the Hebrew, *raah*. The following will be a piece of information for future lexicographers.

"*Scopeo*, the original Greek word, in those texts, (Phil. ii. 4.; 2 Cor. iv. 18,) neither signifies *look upon*, nor *look at*, but HEED, MIND, or REGARD; and is, therefore, nothing to the purpose of illustrating the text in Proverbs, ('Look not upon the wine,') which refers to physical seeing; as indeed, anybody might see, with half-an-eye, if he but cared to look at the context." (p. 14.)

The peculiar genius which breathes in the Reply is no where more clearly displayed than here. *Scopeo*, says our Critic, means not, *look upon*: it means, *to regard*. It does not mean, *to look at*: but *to heed*. All this may explain some things which certainly needed explanation. The Doctor seems ripe for the confession that what his eyes have *seen*, his mind has not *regarded*, and that he has given *heed* to something, which he has imagined to be in the Bible, but which neither he nor any one else has seen there. All this is too possible: but it is scarcely conceivable that all the lexicons, and literal readings are wrong, which declare *scopeo* to signify, *look, watch, behold, look at or upon*.

"Nor does the Hebrew word anywhere mean 'inordinate desire,' but *to see*; whether *pain* or *pleasure* are connoted, the context alone can determine.—(Ps. liv. 7; Gen. xxi. 16.) Mr. Williams should have looked upon these and similar texts, where the same word occurs in the original as well as in the version." (p. 15.)

The design of all this is to show, if possible, that my comparing Prov. xxiii. 31, with 2 Cor. iv. 18, and Phil. ii. 4, fails to establish what was indicated in my lecture, p. 38. It is there asked: "Does not the expression, *look not*, in these passages, signify that we are not to look upon the things which are referred to *with inordinate desire and affection*." It is quite true that neither the Hebrew *raah*, in the Old Testament, nor the Greek *scopeo*, in the New, signifies *by itself*, inordinate desire. In either case, the context alone must decide with regard to the desire or hatred. *Scopeo* certainly refers in the New Testament to an attentive consideration of the object. But in this it is only the equivalent of the Hebrew *raah*, which is also used in many places to denote, not, as the Doctor would say, a physical seeing, but *attentive consideration*. Let us regard the following passages, in all of which we have the same verb, which is rendered in Prov. xxiii. 31, *look upon*, translated, *look to, see to, see, have experience of, enjoy, behold.*—Gen. xxxix. 23. "The commander of the prison-house *attended* to (looked to) nothing which was in his (Joseph's) hand."—Ps. xxxiv. 8. "Taste and *consider* (see) that Jehovah is good."—Ps. xlix. 10. "For he *observeth* (seeth) that the wise die."—Ps. liii. 2. "God from heaven stooped above the sons of man, to *observe* (see) if there were one that had understanding."—Eccl. i. 16. "And my heart *was attentive* (had experience) to increase wisdom and knowledge." —Eccl. ix. 9. "*Enjoy* life (live joyfully, or as it is in the margin, *see* life) with the wife whom thou lovest."—Isa. xxvi. 10. "In the land of righteousness he will act unrighteously, and will not *regard* (behold) the majesty of Jehovah." In all these texts, and many others, we are bound to take the Hebrew *raah* as signifying what our Critic acknowledges to be the meaning of the Greek *scopeo*. The one word is in fact the equivalent of the other. Then what does our Critic mean, if not to hide himself by a dexterous manœuvre, or a most atrocious bungling with Hebrew and Greek, when, in face of the facts which are stated, he can write as follows?

"Mr. Williams is plainly arguing on the English phrase alone, which renders his logic all the more ridiculous, since it does not follow that because, in different texts, the words of the translation are the same, those of the original are." (p. 14.)

Does the Replier suppose that we are so benighted as not to know that the word in Proverbs is Hebrew, and that which is employed in the Epistles to Corinth and Philippi, is Greek?

"Our Critic has fallen into another pit—a most righteous Nemesis for his endeavour to obscure a plain text and a plain important truth. He has actually cited in illustration two texts which do not contain the equivalents of the English words at all!" (p. 14.)

Don't be deceived, Doctor: an avenging Nemesis never misses the true mark. If I have been guilty of an improper comparison or inference, I am willing to submit in this matter to the verdict of such as are capable of deciding fairly. But if the Hebrew word in Prov. xxiii. 31, is, after all, synonymous with the Greek in the New Testament passages referred to, then it is *your* logic that will appear ridiculous, not mine. It may be repeated, however, that if *scopeo* means *heed, mind,* or *regard,* so does the Hebrew *raah;* and therefore we may read the passage in Proverbs as follows:—" *Heed not* the wine, or *do not thou regard it,* when it is red." True, there will not be much loss or gain to Dr. Lees by such a rendering; the difference being so unimportant between the expressions, *look not,* and *heed not,* that it would scarcely be worthy of a thought, except for the purpose of raising a cloud of dust, behind which our Critic might hide the leanness of his argument. We are quite willing to accept our Critic's own paraphrase, which he gives us on the 15th page of the Reply, as follows:—

"Do not thou look upon the wine with desire."

No doubt this is the meaning of the passage. The force of the recommendation is precisely the same as when a father says to his tippling son: Don't be greedy of your wine, boy! Wherever the advice comes from, it is equally sensible. But father Bottle-nose might shake his sides merrily when accused of teaching his son Teetotalism. Why, he says, I only told him not to be greedy.

Our Critic's warning is very important when he refers to the "danger of being ensnared *into* habits of profligacy." We will give him credit for stating *that* more distinctly than it is declared in the Book of Proverbs. True, "it is best to lock the door before the mare is stolen." But to do so we should not need to go to the Bible for a written injunction.

> "We deny, however, most emphatically, that either Paul or Solomon has anywhere ascribed evil to natural Food, or to the proper things of the world, or that they have imperatively warned us that we must not *look upon them* (with desire); nevertheless they have *both* plainly taught abstinence from strong drink, on the ground of its being essentially evil in its relations to man." (p. 15.)

But the emphasis of our Critic's asseveration or denial will not alter *the fact*, that both Paul and Solomon have ascribed as much evil to artificial food as to artificial drink, and have no more plainly taught abstinence from strong drink than from anything else which causes to offend. But what is there, that does not, at one time or another, become the innocent occasion of offence? Paul plainly enjoins abstinence from meat, if that should cause a brother to offend, or even to suffer grief. "If thy brother be grieved on account of thy meat, now walkest thou not according to charity. Destroy not him with thy meat for whom Christ died.......Do not, for the sake of meat, destroy the work of God. All things indeed are pure; but it is evil in the man who eateth so as to give offence. It is good neither to eat flesh, nor to drink wine, nor anything whereby thy brother stumbleth, or is offended, or is made weak. Happy is he who condemneth not himself in what he approveth. For he who is in strife with himself, is condemned if he eat, because it is not from faith: for all that is not from faith is sin."—(Rom. xiv. 15, 20—23.) We are aware that, in these verses, Paul is treating of ceremonial objections to the use of certain kinds of food which were proscribed under the Jewish law. But that does not alter the state of the case with regard to our argument. The principle is clearly expressed, that we are to choose what we shall eat and drink according to the dictates of conscience. We must maintain our Christian liberty. "Let every man be fully persuaded in his own mind."—(Rom. xiv. 5.) But at the same time, we must act charitably, not grieving any brother with our meat. Does all this plainly teach Teetotalism? Then it also plainly teaches Vegetarianism: for the consciences of our vegetarian brothers are sometimes offended at our eating animal food. Both our consciences and our stomachs might be offended by some of the dainties of our continental neighbours, or with the confections of some at home.

But what are the true circumstances, under which it is declared that Paul has "plainly taught abstinence from strong drink"? Dr. Lees' lecture, it is said, "establishes the seven propositions" by which Teetotalism was to be represented as the plain teaching of the Bible, "upon the plain words of the authorized version, and carefully avoids *critical* disquisition founded on the original Hebrew." (See quotation from the Reply, p. 55.) After such a boast, we might have expected, at least, that the Doctor would establish his propositions as to the Teetotalism of the New Testament in a similar way. But what is the direct teaching of our English New Testament concerning Teetotalism? The Doctor seems to be silent on this. At the conclusion of his pamphlet entitled, "Teetotalism in its relations to the New Testament," we observe the following:— "Thus do the varied language of the New Testament, and the known facts of antiquity, conspire to establish our critical theory." *Critical* enough. The language employed by Dr. Lees to express the meaning of Paul in the New Testament, is certainly *varied* from our English versions more than enough. But, it would seem, not enough to please the Doctor; and so we find expressions, said to convey Paul's meaning, *variegated* with quotations from heathen writers, who may be expected to have great weight with some who never read them, inasmuch as Dr. Lees says that they *conspire* with the New Testament, or the New Testament with them, to establish his critical theory. 'Tis a marvellous conspiracy! Our suspicion is, that the said Dr. Lees is at the bottom as well as the top of it.

But having looked at the end, let us turn to the beginning, and we shall see that the argument for the New Testament teaching is commenced in as rickety a fashion as it concludes. "IF TEETOTALISM," says our Author, "BE so variously and persistently taught in the Law and Prophets of the Jew, can it be quite contradicted and discarded in the gospel of the Christian?" Undoubtedly if we could be brought to believe in Teetotalism as the law of the Pentateuch, the teaching of the Proverbs, and the hope of the Prophets, we might expect that it would be neither contradicted nor discarded in the New Testament. But to show that it is *plainly taught* in the New Testament requires something beside the bare negation that it is not contradicted there.

We are told, however, that there are certain Greek terms which inculcate abstinence. One of these is said to be "EGKRATEIA, *temperance*." "This," says Dr. Lees, " is the correct rendering of the Greek in its general sense, but it had likewise the meaning of *abstinence* from sensual gratification . . . . The law which enjoins the performance of right actions, equally demands *abstinence* from bad ones." But who is to decide that the drinking of a small quantity of fermented wine is always and necessarily a bad moral action? If the Doctor can so far succeed in altering the standard of Christian morality as to convince people that it is, in every case, the violation of a law, either Divine or human, to take strong drink, then we shall admit that the New Testament teaches total abstinence. But that, so far as I am aware, is not even the teaching of Teetotalism. And if it be neither the teaching of Teetotalism nor the Bible, then whose teaching is it? Is it the teaching of Science? No: for medical science says: there are cases in which the human constitution absolutely requires wine for the prolonging of life: and social science urges that Teetotalism is a special expedient for special times and circumstances. Then what is the teaching of the New Testament *egkrateia*, or temperance? Plainly, *temperance;* or the lawful use of what is good in its proper place, and at the proper time. But the word itself teaches nothing as to *what is* the proper place and time. The decision of that it leaves to the teachings of science and our ordinary perception of things. Then the word *egkrateia* does not teach Teetotalism.

But Dr. Lees proceeds to show that the Apostles *explicitly* enjoin the practice of Teetotalism. The Greek word *nēphaleos* or *nēphalios* is rendered in our English New Testament as follows: 1 Tim. iii. 2, 'vigilant': 1 Tim. iii. 11, and Tit. ii. 2, 'sober'. If the word is to be understood in its common usage, Paul plainly teaches by these passages that bishops, wives of deacons, and old men must be *sober*. Dr. Lees, however, would render the term: '*abstinent from wine.*' But the distinction between perfect sobriety and abstinence from wine is not a very wide one, unless the Doctor means by abstinence, *total abstinence*, and that always. But he has no sufficient authority for affirming that Paul meant the latter. That any passage in the New Testament distinctly teaches by the term *nēphalios*, total abstinence from strong drink, may be the plain teaching of Dr. Lees; but he will scarcely expect that many persons, who are at all acquainted with the Greek, will accept such teaching as genuine.

A kindred word *nēphō* or *nēphōn* is used in six New Testament passages, where we have the English rendering thus.—1 Th. v. 6, 8; 1 Pet. i. 13; v. 8; 'be sober:' 2 Tim. iv. 5; 1 Pet. iv. 7; 'watch.' To the word which is here in the original, Dr. Lees would apply, instead of the proper rendering, *be sober*, an etymological sense which was probably obsolete in the times of the apostles; *viz. drink not*. We hope, that the Doctor will not be guilty of suicide by following the very plain injunction which such a rendering would impose. That the passages just referred to teach Teetotalism is mere conjecture at the utmost. To multitudes it will appear a very wild conjecture. One of our most eminent Greek Lexicographers has said in a private letter: "The words *nēphōn, nēphalios* primarily refer no doubt to *abstinence from wine*, but that this implies *total abstinence* would be rash to affirm, and as difficult as most negations are to prove."

The words *mē paroinos*, as used in 1 Tim. iii. 3; Tit. i. 7, are regarded by Dr. Lees as conveying an injunction to Bishops *not to come near to* wine. Where we read: "not given to wine;" we are required to read: "not near wine." If Dr. Lees' rendering is the right one, the injunction, not to come near wine, would apply in all its force to Timothy, who was himself a Bishop; and Paul is made at once to contradict himself, for before the epistle is concluded, in which Bishops are thus enjoined not to be near wine, Timothy is told to use a little. (ch. v. 23.) But I will quote again the words of a scholar who, I venture to think, is much more competent to pronounce a judgment on the word *paroinos* than Dr. Lees. "*Paroinos* means, *given to make a wrong use of wine*, according to a common sense of *para* in composition, as PARAKOPTO, *to stamp* coin *with a false dye*; PARASĒMOS, *falsely marked, counterfeit*, etc." Dr. Lees quotes Robinson as follows: "PAROINOS, *by wine;* by or over wine." But on turning to Robinson's Greek

Lexicon, we find that Dr. Lees has not quoted fully. The quotation should be thus:—" PAROINOS, *by wine*, i.e. spoken of what takes place *by* or over wine, revelry. In N. T. of persons, i.q. *given to wine*, p.p. sitting long by wine."

Now it must be evident to any thoughtful mind, that a positive injunction for Teetotalism in the New Testament cannot be established on such premises as we have been considering. Dr. Lees himself gives up the New Testament teaching of total abstinence when he says in "Teetotalism—its Relations to the New Test." (p. 95) as follows:—" It is somewhat remarkable, that 1 Tim. iii. 3, and Tit. i. 7, exhibit the word *paroinos*, i.e. *vinosus, sitting at wine*, in reference to Bishops; while 1 Tim. iii. 8, and Titus ii. 3, both in reference to Deacons, use the phrase *much wine, oinos polus*...... The *deacons* may use wine, but not *much* wine; but the *bishops* must not be *paroinoi*." Again we read on the same page: "Paul, it seems clear, desired the Bishops not to be present in wine feasts. ....When he wished to speak against *excess* of wine, he knew perfectly well how to express himself. He says, 'Likewise must the Deacons be grave,.........not having the countenance towards *much* wine' (1 Tim. iii. 8)—and 'The aged women (not *deacons*, nor *deaconesses*, as the Doctor elsewhere insists) likewise,......not slanderers, *not enslaved to* MUCH wine' (Tit. ii. 3.)." "Not *overpowered* by much wine," is another rendering which has come under our notice elsewhere, and equally correct with the expression, *not enslaved*: both, however, implying a permission to use wine in moderation.

To the same effect are the numerous denunciations against drunkenness in the Word of God. If taking the first drop were the sin, why should the Bible affix its brand so emphatically on the *drunkard?* Gluttony and drunkenness are condemned together as kindred vices, and with them other forms of intemperance, as intemperate desire, and intemperate speech. "Be not deceived; God is not mocked: for whatsoever a man soweth, that shall he also reap. For he that soweth to his flesh shall of the flesh reap corruption; but he that soweth to the Spirit shall of the Spirit reap life everlasting."

THE END.

www.ingramcontent.com/pod-product-compliance
Ingram Content Group UK Ltd.
Pitfield, Milton Keynes, MK11 3LW, UK
UKHW041950230426
12048UKWH00008B/250